T0053360

To:

....

From:

....

Praise for Karen Ehman and Ruth Schwenk

"Just one moment with Jesus is enough for our hearts to be transformed forever. *Pressing Pause* creates a space for this type of life-changing encounter to take place. In this collection of thought-provoking and heart-mending truth, Karen and Ruth have created an opportunity for women in any stage of life to meet with Jesus. Surely there is no sweeter thing."
> —Becky Thompson, author of *Hope Unfolding*
> and founder of Scissortail SILK

"*Pressing Pause* is perfectly portioned for busy moms, ideal for a morning devotion or a quick perspective shift in the middle of a crazy day. Ruth and Karen understand the challenges of motherhood and speak right to the heart with truth, humor, and hope."
> —Kat Lee, speaker and writer at InspiredToAction.com

"Too often moms get caught up in the daily chaos of managing home life, work, and children. Ruth and Karen meet their readers where they are in the hard reality of life—gently leading them to a God who waits to sit and give them rest."
> —Sandra E. Maddox, founder and coordinator of Treasured
> Moms Ministry at Saddleback Church, author of *Tiffany and
> The Talking Frog*, and blogger at TheArtofDomesticity.com

"*Hoodwinked* reads like an encouraging letter from a friend. It is full of grace, biblical wisdom, and inspiration. Many books on motherhood leave me wondering if I'm doing it all wrong. Karen and Ruth are bravely transparent and meet us moms right where we are. This book gives us the hope and encouragement we need in the midst of weary days."
> —Courtney Joseph, author and blogger at WomenLivingWell.org,
> home of Good Morning Girls

"Karen and Ruth understand what it is to battle the voices of guilt, anxiety, and inadequacy that plague many mothers who want to give their best to their children. In *Hoodwinked*, they share life-changing truths that all mothers can grab hold of, not just to survive the journey of motherhood but to thrive in confidence and joy."
> —Chrystal Evans Hurst, bestselling author of *She's Still There*

"Karen Ehman's blog was one of the first I ever read, and she's never stopped being a mentor to me. Her words here speak my heart language—and echo the heart of God."

—ANN VOSKAMP, *NEW YORK TIMES* BESTSELLING AUTHOR
OF *ONE THOUSAND GIFTS* AND *THE BROKEN WAY*

"Ruth Schwenk is an ambassador for us moms in the trenches. She knows the worries that weigh heavily on our hearts, and she gets the mom guilt that threatens to steal the joy from our parenting journeys. And she is passionate about helping us grow *through* it and find freedom *in* it."

—JEANNIE CUNNION, AUTHOR OF *MOM SET FREE*

"A teacher at heart, Karen skillfully weaves together biblical examples, hard-earned wisdom, and real-life stories to create a resource our world desperately needs."

—LIZ CURTIS HIGGS, BESTSELLING AUTHOR OF *THE GIRL'S STILL GOT IT*

"Through vulnerability and sharing personal stories of her own motherhood journey, Ruth inspires moms to intentionally pursue becoming better moms as we all seek to be more like Christ. Ruth's stories of motherhood and marriage are relatable, letting us know that none of us is really alone in our struggles."

—JENNIFER SMITH, AUTHOR OF *THE UNVEILED WIFE* AND *WIFE AFTER GOD*

"Karen Ehman is a breath of fresh air. She provides faith-filled inspiration and practical ideas for taking notice of others, using our words wisely, and scattering God's kindness in an often negative world. I wish every one of my social media followers would listen to and follow the advice in her Keep It Shut message."

—CANDACE CAMERON BURE, *NEW YORK TIMES* BESTSELLING
AUTHOR, ACTRESS, AND PRODUCER

"Ruth's [writing] will give you a counselor to listen to, a friend to walk beside you, and an experienced voice from someone who has learned to seek God's grace and truth every step of motherhood."

—SALLY CLARKSON, SPEAKER, BLOGGER, PODCASTER, AND AUTHOR
OF NUMEROUS BESTSELLING BOOKS INCLUDING *THE MISSION OF
MOTHERHOOD*, *DESPERATE*, AND *THE LIFEGIVING HOME*

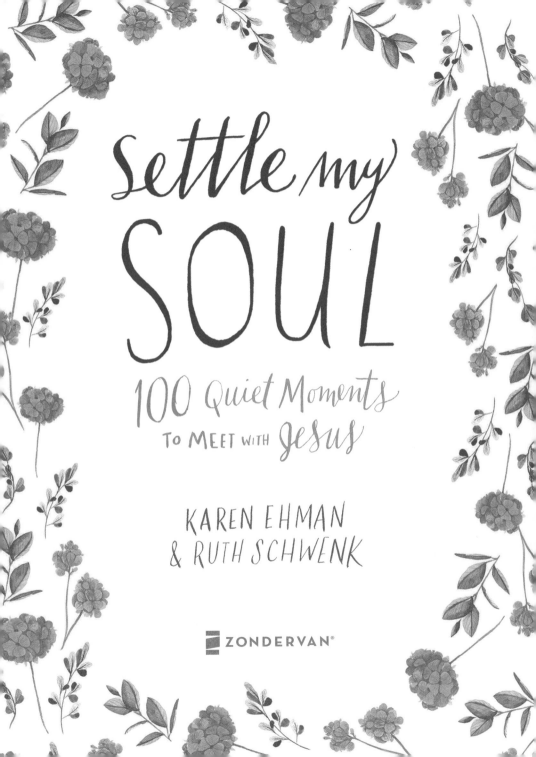

settle my SOUL

100 Quiet Moments TO MEET WITH Jesus

KAREN EHMAN & RUTH SCHWENK

ZONDERVAN®

ZONDERVAN
Settle My Soul

© 2019 by Karen Ehman and Ruth Schwenk

Published in Grand Rapids, Michigan, by Zondervan. Zondervan is a registered trademark of The Zondervan Corporation, L.L.C., a wholly owned subsidiary of HarperCollins Christian Publishing, Inc.

Requests for information should be addressed to customercare@harpercollins.com.

ISBN 978-0-310-13977-5 (audiobook)
ISBN 978-0-310-09541-5 (eBook)
ISBN 978-0-310-09540-8 (HC)

Unless otherwise noted, Scripture quotations are taken from the Holy Bible, New International Version®, NIV®. Copyright © 1973, 1978, 1984, 2011 by Biblica, Inc.® Used by permission of Zondervan. All rights reserved worldwide. www.Zondervan.com. The "NIV" and "New International Version" are trademarks registered in the United States Patent and Trademark Office by Biblica, Inc.®

Scripture quotations marked AMP are from the Amplified® Bible. Copyright © 1954, 1958, 1962, 1964, 1965, 1987 by The Lockman Foundation. Used by permission. www.Lockman.org

Scripture quotations marked ESV are from the ESV® Bible (The Holy Bible, English Standard Version®). Copyright © 2001 by Crossway, a publishing ministry of Good News Publishers. Used by permission. All rights reserved. ·

Scripture quotations marked CSB are from the Christian Standard Bible®. Copyright © 2017 by Holman Bible Publishers. Used by permission. Christian Standard Bible®, and CSB® are federally registered trademarks of Holman Bible Publishers, all rights reserved.

Scripture quotations marked KJV are from the King James Version, public domain.

Scripture quotations marked NLT are from the Holy Bible, New Living Translation. Copyright © 1996, 2004, 2007, 2013, 2015 by Tyndale House Foundation. Used by permission of Tyndale House Ministries, Carol Stream, Illinois 60188. All rights reserved.

Any internet addresses (websites, blogs, etc.) and telephone numbers in this book are offered as a resource. They are not intended in any way to be or imply an endorsement by Zondervan, nor does Zondervan vouch for the content of these sites and numbers for the life of this book.

All rights reserved. No part of this publication may be reproduced, stored in a retrieval system, or transmitted in any form or by any means—electronic, mechanical, photocopy, recording, or any other—except for brief quotations in printed reviews, without the prior permission of the publisher.

Authors are represented by the literary agency of The Fedd Agency, Inc., P. O. Box 34173, Austin, Texas 78734

Art direction: Adam Hill
Interior design: Lori Lynch

To Courtney, for showing us how to let Jesus settle
our souls, no matter what life may bring

Contents

CONTENTS

CONTENTS

CONTENTS

CONTENTS

Introduction

Hi, friend. Is your day jam-packed with obligations and never-ending to-do lists? If you're anything like us, the answer is yes! If so, start here: Turn off your phone notifications. Ignore the dirty laundry for a little longer. Stop thinking about the work project that's on a tight deadline or what you're going to cook for dinner tonight. If these things leave you feeling frazzled, what you need most isn't better time-management skills or tips for worrying less—you need a settled soul.

As busy women juggling lots of responsibilities just like you, we know how hard it can be to press pause and refresh your spirit. Yet it's crucial that you do! Whether you're a working professional, a wife, a mom, a sister, an aunt, a student, or any combination of these things, your stressed and exhausted heart needs time carved out for God.

Through the 100 devotions found in the book you hold in your hands, it is our prayer that each devotion meets you where you are and cuts through the noise of your busy life. So take a few quiet moments to meet with Jesus. Ponder the scripture, insights learned, and questions for reflection meant to help you connect your heart straight to God's.

As you spend a little time savoring the Savior and align your thoughts with His Word before you head out to meet the demands of the day, may you discover what Jesus longs to give you: His peace.

In His incredible love,
Karen and Ruth

1

How to Scatter Unusual Kindness

Karen

*Once safely on shore, we found out that the island was called
Malta. The islanders showed us unusual kindness. They built
a fire and welcomed us all because it was raining and cold.*

—ACTS 28:1–2

*H*ave you ever read a story on social media about someone who did something over-the-top for a stranger? Like tipping a restaurant server not just the standard 20 percent, but maybe 500 percent? I love stories like these, and we don't just find them online.

Tucked in the pages of the New Testament is a two-word phrase that seemed to leap off the pages of my Bible one day. It rearranged my thinking and became a life mission.

In Acts 28:1–2, we encounter some unknown people who lived on a remote island where a boatload of people—including the apostle Paul—suddenly found themselves shipwrecked in the middle of a storm: "Once safely on shore, we found out that the island was called Malta. The islanders showed us unusual kindness."

Unusual kindness.

I love the reason given for this above-and-beyond behavior. These verses don't say this unusual kindness was shown because Paul and his companions were important people. It doesn't declare, "The people from the shipwreck had the exact political and theological views as the islanders." No, they were treated with this unusual kindness simply because "it was raining and cold."

Today we encounter all sorts of people who are up against the elements. We can't always see these circumstances, but they are present nonetheless. Perhaps those people could use some kindness—even better, unusual kindness.

Kindness holds the door for an elderly person leaving the grocery store. Unusual kindness willingly carries the person's groceries all the way to her car, puts them in the trunk, and sends her on her way with an "It was my pleasure" when thanked.

Kindness is smiling at the maxed-out mom with two kids who are pitching fits in the coffee shop line rather than staring in silence. Unusual kindness tells her to hang in there because she's doing an important job and then pays for her coffee.

Kindness whispers a prayer for the just-moved-in neighbor who's facing life all alone. Unusual kindness invites him to your house for a weekend supper, folds him into your family's ordinary life, and asks questions to get to know him better.

Scatter some unusual kindness today. When you do, you'll make someone else's day—and yours!

> Father, as I encounter people today, help me remember the
> example of the islanders of Malta and show others unusual
> kindness done in Your name. In Jesus' name, amen.

∞ In the space provided, brainstorm a few "unusual kindness"
   ideas for the people in your life.

2

Rethinking Solitude

Very early in the morning, while it was still dark, Jesus got up, left
the house and went off to a solitary place, where he prayed.

—MARK 1:35

I never fully understood, or appreciated, the discipline of solitude until well into adulthood. Sure, I had studied about growing in Christ by reading God's Word, memorizing scripture, devoting time to prayer, and serving others. But solitude always puzzled me, especially as an extrovert.

Who wants to be alone? I love people. I have always found myself energized by being with others, not by getting away from them! And then life, with all its joy and demands, began to open my eyes to the importance of getting alone.

What had once seemed strange to me suddenly began to feel like a necessity. I rediscovered passages like Mark 1:35. Jesus, after a long and demanding day, started His new day by getting up and getting alone—He practiced solitude. If Jesus needed solitude, surely I do too.

But God has been showing me lately that I have only partially understood the importance of solitude. Many of us tend to view solitude as *our* time away. It's time to be alone with God. To hear from Him. To be refreshed. And while all this is true, I missed an important part of solitude. Alone time is not the end goal. It is a means to something far more important, something that Jesus taught was the greatest commandment: to love God and love others.

In other words, solitude is not primarily about withdrawing *from* people, but withdrawing *for* people. Jesus withdrew for the sake of reengaging people to love, heal, and bless them. Solitude does require that we get alone, but we do it so when we reengage with family, friends, or coworkers, we are the kind of people who love others well.

Solitude is not just for us; solitude is for the sake of others.

Father, my soul finds rest in You alone. You renew me with Your love, grace, and truth. Help me cultivate the discipline of solitude, not just for my sake, but for the sake of others. Remind me that my times of getting alone with You are ultimately meant to move me closer to others—to bring life, healing, truth, and hope to those You surround me with. In Jesus' name, amen.

- What is one way you can begin cultivating the discipline of solitude in your own life?
- What are the top one or two obstacles you need to overcome to practice times of being alone?

....

....

....

....

....

3

Hang On a Second

Karen

I assure you, believers, by the pride which I have in you in [your union with] Christ Jesus our Lord, I die daily [I face death and die to self].

—1 CORINTHIANS 15:31 AMP

When he was a middle schooler, my youngest son had a fondness for iPod games where a creature had to jump, twist, dodge, and dart in an effort to stay alive. Often he played them on our short commute to school each morning.

As we drove, we'd go over pick-up instructions. I'd also give my *"Be sure your sins will find you out"* lecture that my own sweet mama often gave me. My son would just keep playing his game, acting as if he wasn't listening. But I knew he was.

Often when jockeying for a position in the carpool line, I'd inform my boy that it was time to get out of the vehicle. Usually, still engaged in the game, he would utter the same phrase to me: "Hang on a second. I gotta die." As in, "I don't want to quit just yet. Let my character finish this round until it dies. Then I will get out of the car."

As he said it one morning, it spoke to my soul.

As a follower of Christ, I am to die to self. But so often I do not. I elevate self. I promote self. I think little of the other person and much of myself. But before I react, before I hurl a harsh word, before I pass judgment or speak unkindly, perhaps I need to take a deep breath. To pause and ponder. To say in a spiritual sense, "Hang on a second. I gotta die."

How do we learn to die to self in the everyday details of life? These daily, hourly, and even moment-by-moment decisions are difficult! If we try to die to self out of our own strength, it will seem impossible. In these times, we must draw deep from the power the Holy Spirit offers and let His proper response override our natural and sinful one.

So the next time we want to react in a way that won't please God, let's remember my game-lovin' guy and *before* we speak, take a deep breath. Take a pause that centers our heart, snaps our soul to attention, and gently declares, "Hang on a second. I gotta die."

Dear Lord, may I learn to die daily. To both act and react in a way that pleases You. In Jesus' name, amen.

❧ What are some places or situations in which God is asking you to press pause and give yourself a minute to consider how your actions might affect others?

....

....

....

....

....

....

4

Is God at Work in My Life?

If I rise on the wings of the dawn, if I settle on the far side of the sea,
even there your hand will guide me, your right hand will hold me fast.

—PSALM 139:9–10

Our world was turned upside down not too long ago. After a series of tests, doctors finally diagnosed my husband with a type of blood cancer. As we wrestled with the initial news, my mind darted in a million different directions. Every emotion exploded inside me. I felt fear, insecurity, and even anger.

God, what are You doing? I said to myself. *This happens to other people. Not me.* And yet, as much as I resisted, my husband and I were instantly thrust into a new season of life, a different kind of journey than we ever imagined or wanted. This was our life. Whether I liked it or not, I was forced to answer the question, "Is God really at work in *this*?"

When life is not going the way I want it to, it's easy for me to get angry. I can begin to make moral judgments about how life should and shouldn't work. In essence, I am saying I can better plan my life than God can! I can be tempted to think God is indifferent, absent, or cruel. So anger can often reveal when my heart is not trusting, waiting, and believing in God's power to accomplish what He wants to in, and through, my life.

Through my husband's cancer diagnosis, I am learning to trust God in new ways. As my heart gets exposed, my faith is expanding. Even in the midst of trials, I am learning that God really is at work in my life. When I am tempted to be angry or resentful, God reminds me that He is good, His purposes never fail, and like today's verse says, His hand will guide me (Psalm 139:10).

What are you going through right now? Are you tempted to doubt God's goodness or activity in your life? Is your anger revealing a heart that doubts God's presence and purpose? I pray that God would give you wisdom and faith to walk with Him, leaning on Him even in the storms.

> Father, I trust You. I know You are good and faithful. I surrender my plans to You, knowing that Your purposes never fail. Give me faith to trust You and obey You even when I don't understand what is going on. I believe You are with me and for me. In Jesus' name, amen.

❧ How has doubting God's presence led to your becoming angry?
❧ In what area of your life are you most tempted to doubt God's work?

....

....

....

....

....

....

5

Go Find Your Old Self

Karen

Praise be to the God and Father of our Lord Jesus Christ, the
Father of compassion and the God of all comfort, who comforts
us in all our troubles, so that we can comfort those in any
trouble with the comfort we ourselves receive from God.

—2 CORINTHIANS 1:3–4

I sat on my twin-sized bed, curled up in my lavender bedspread, sobbing until I felt I had no tears left. My eleven-year-old self once again had her hopes dashed, causing a wave of grief that would only subside once exhaustion set in and sleep took over.

Over the years, the four walls of my bedroom witnessed the heart cries of a young girl trying desperately to navigate relationships, reality, and a new normal.

Toward the end of high school, I became connected to the little country church across the street where I was told the gospel story. I responded to the Spirit's invitation and placed my trust in Jesus. Becoming a believer didn't change my circumstances. But it *did* change my response to them.

As I spent time with my mentor from the church, Miss Pat, I saw where to take my sorrow, how to deal with my grief, and how to find comfort in the security of God's love.

Today's passage, 2 Corinthians 1:3–4, is a picture of this very concept.

As Miss Pat thought about the ways God had comforted her in the past, she reached out to me with that same comfort, helping me deal with the various situations life brought my way. She pointed me to the Father of compassion.

Today, as a mother of teenagers and young adults, I often find myself in a situation similar to hers. In many ways I feel that by ministering to the people God sends my way, I am being like Miss Pat was to me. I am comforting others with the comfort I myself have received from Christ.

If you feel your past hurts lack purpose, I have a very simple solution: Go find a version of your old self and encourage her. Comfort her. Love her. Point her to Christ. When you do, you will find purpose in your past pain. And you'll be an example to someone who just might keep the circle of comfort going.

Father, thank You for being my hope and comforting me in
all my troubles. May I encourage others with the stories
of Your faithfulness to me. In Jesus' name, amen.

ॐ Who is your old self? Describe her below. Describe how you would have liked to have been comforted at that time in your life. Tuck this away in your mind, and commit to seeking out this old version of you. When you find her, love her well.

....

....

....

....

6

Reordering Our Thoughts

Ruth

"Keep this Book of the Law always on your lips; meditate on it day and night, so that you may be careful to do everything written in it. Then you will be prosperous and successful."

—JOSHUA 1:8

What consumes your thoughts most days? When given the chance, where does your mind wander? Are you frequently overwhelmed with worry or stress? One of the best things to do when that happens is meditate on God's truth and love.

In the Bible we quickly discover that God changes us by changing how we think—through the reordering of our thoughts. In Joshua 1:8, we are told to guard God's Word. Keep it close to our lips and mediate on it day and night.

Meditating is not the absence of thinking; meditation is the act of thinking rightly. When God instructs us to meditate, He is not asking us to empty our thoughts, but rather to focus our thoughts on Him. To meditate on God's Word is to measure it carefully, thinking about a verse or passage over and over again. It is to keep coming back to God's Word and fixing our hearts and minds on the goodness of what God is offering us.

As we meditate on God's Word, we can allow God to change us by:

- Thinking about what is excellent or praiseworthy (Philippians 4:8).
- Allowing our minds to be controlled by the Holy Spirit (Romans 8:6).
- Feeding our minds regularly with the truth of God's Word (Romans 12:1–2).
- Resting and reflecting on God's promises (Psalm 62:1–2).
- Praying God's Word (Nehemiah 9:6–37).

Maybe instead of reading four or five chapters of your Bible today, God wants to you to slow down and meditate on just one verse. Let it soak in. Fight off every lie that is attacking your mind. Order your thoughts around what is true. Allow God to change you by changing your thoughts!

Father, Your Word is a lamp unto my feet. Teach me to slow down and fix my thoughts on Your truth today. Guard my thoughts from doubt, discouragement, and lies. Fill my mind with Your Word, and allow my thinking to be controlled by Your Spirit so I might experience greater life and peace. In Jesus' name, amen.

- Where do you struggle most with your thinking right now?
- How can you begin to meditate on God's Word today?

....

....

....

....

7

Know the Whole Story

Karen

> *Jesus said to the Jews who had believed him, "If you*
> *continue in my word, you really are my disciples. You will*
> *know the truth, and the truth will set you free."*

—JOHN 8:31–32 CSB

*D*o you remember your very first job? My most-loved young-adult job was when I spent two summers at a nature center teaching classes for four-year-olds. I learned how to identify critters in the pond, how to tell a chipmunk from a thirteen-lined ground squirrel, and—of utmost importance—how to spot poison ivy.

My poison ivy identification skills have come in handy over the years. One time a friend suspected she had it growing all over her shed. Upon inspection, I discovered she was right. So her family took care to remove it, wearing long sleeves and gloves for protection.

But then she mentioned they'd burned all the ivy in a giant bonfire while they stood over it roasting marshmallows . . . Oh no!

While my friend knew the danger of touching the ivy itself, it hadn't occurred to her that burning the plant—creating smoke that had the plant's oils mingled in it—would cause a worse reaction than just touching the leaves.

Sure enough, her whole family developed blistering rashes, especially on their faces, and their eyes became sorely bloodshot and painfully itchy. One son even developed a serious respiratory reaction. All this occurred because she only knew half the truth about poison ivy: that touching it is bad. She didn't know that burning it is even worse.

Like the Jews in today's passage who "had believed" in Jesus (John 8:31 CSB), the beginning of our walks with God is only half of the story. But we can't stop there. We must keep growing in Christ, continually walking in God's Word in a way that sets us free and keeps sin from poisoning our lives and causing a mighty, even painful, mess.

Jesus saved us (past tense), but He is continually perfecting us too (present tense) if only we will cooperate.

What a glorious thought: We can know the truth. The truth sets us free. How? "If you continue in my word" (v. 31 CSB).

Don't live half the story just by believing in Jesus. Keep going and growing into maturity.

> Father, help me not just rest in my belief in You, but also
> continue in Your Word to find the truth-giving life You
> offer me through Your Son. In Jesus' name, amen.

∞ For you, what tends to get in the way of continuing in God's Word? Busyness? Laziness? Poor time management? What one change can you strive to make that will allow you to better spend time in God's Word?

....

....

....

8

The God Who Loves Us

Ruth

May your unfailing love be with us, Lord, even as we put our hope in you.

—PSALM 33:22

Psalm 33 is a beautiful song of praise. It moves from praising God for His Word, justice, and faithfulness to recounting the story of God's mighty acts of creation. The psalmist praised God for keeping His promises and rejoiced in the assurance that God is our King. No matter what we are going through, we can meet God in praise and "wait in hope for the Lord; he is our help and our shield" (Psalm 33:20).

But as the psalmist comes to a close, he does not end with God's unfailing power, incomprehensible wisdom, or unrivaled glory. He has all those things, to be sure. No one is like Him. Despite many contenders, He has no rivals. The Lord is mighty, wise, good, and glorious. But in today's passage, the psalmist appealed to God's unfailing love: "May your unfailing love be with us, Lord, even as we put our hope in you" (v. 22).

God's is a kind of love that never ends. It doesn't run out or fall short, even when we do. God's love is the real thing. It is better than the highest praise from people. God is truly the only One who knows us completely yet loves us the most.

If you struggle with believing that God loves you, the real you, look no further than the cross. On the cross, Jesus satisfied God's justice while pouring out His love. Jesus took our place, paying the penalty our sins deserve. By faith, His blood covers us. Washes us clean. Makes us new. Calls us out of hiding. Removes the need to pretend or fake it. We are completely loved with God's unfailing love.

Do you believe that? Is God's unfailing love an anchor for your soul? Or are you still trying to prove yourself to others and to God? I pray that today God's unfailing love would rest on you. That you would know and believe how much He cares for you, is with you, and desires to sustain you.

> Father, I don't just want to know Your love for me; I want to feel Your love. Help me experience Your unconditional love for me in Christ. Give rest to my soul as You teach me about the depths of Your goodness and grace. Your love is what matters most to me. In Jesus' name, amen.

- In what ways do you still try to earn God's love?
- What is one way you can begin to rest in God's love on a daily basis?

....

....

....

....

....

....

....

9

Autocorrected Prayers

Karen

The Spirit helps us in our weakness. For we do not know
what to pray for as we ought, but the Spirit himself
intercedes for us with groanings too deep for words.

—ROMANS 8:26 ESV

I sat at a women's conference table that was charmingly decorated with fresh flowers and laden with delicious food. The conversation flowed as five other women and I chatted about many topics. Most of the ladies were acquaintances, but I hadn't met the woman sitting next to me. "My name is Mem," she said as she introduced herself and we began visiting.

Mem was from another continent. Although her English was excellent, at times she couldn't find the exact word to communicate what she was trying to say.

Several minutes into our conversation, my new friend tried to compliment me on something, but her words didn't convey the proper sentiment. She took a deep breath and with frustration declared, "Oh, Karen. When you cannot understand my words, please hear my heart."

This sweet woman's request has stuck with me since that day, and it's made me think of prayer. There are so many times when I just can't find the right words to say to God.

Tucked in Romans 8:26 (ESV) is a heart-assuring promise: "The Spirit helps us in our weakness. For we do not know what to pray for as we ought, but the Spirit himself intercedes for us with groanings too deep for words." It's like God autocorrects our prayers!

The autocorrect function on a phone or electronic device automatically makes corrections for mistakes in spelling or grammar while we're typing. How comforting it is that the Holy Spirit Himself intercedes for us with groanings too deep for words. When we just can't find the words to pray, God still hears our hearts.

Many times my own emotions have been too deep for words. Each time I trusted that the Holy Spirit would intercede for me, "autocorrecting" my longings and carrying them to the throne of God. I said to Him essentially, "Please hear my heart."

Remember the truth of Romans 8:26, and allow the Spirit of God to intercede on your behalf. God knows you completely—your thoughts, desires, all the inner longings of your heart. Trust that He'll answer your deepest prayers, even when you can't find the right words.

Father, help me pray with boldness, even when I can't find
the words to say, trusting the Spirit to intercede for me and
carry my requests to You. In Jesus' name, amen.

ॐ How might knowing that the Holy Spirit intercedes for you
change the way you personally look at prayer?

....

....

....

10

The Hardest Lessons

Ruth

*Jesus was in the stern, sleeping on a cushion. The disciples woke
him and said to him, "Teacher, don't you care if we drown?"*

—MARK 4:38

We'd done the research. Figured out which boat was best for us.
We even sat in it, paddles in hand, pretending we were in open
water! And then we pulled the trigger and bought our first kayak. The
only problem was that we had never been in the water with one, which is
really the only way to truly learn how to kayak.

We can learn some lessons at the water's edge, but some we have
to learn in the water. This just happens to be the way Jesus taught His
disciples too. In fact, when we begin to read Mark 4, we discover that
"Jesus began to teach by the lake" (v. 1). The crowds gathered, and as they
did, Jesus told them several parables about the kingdom of God.

But then something interesting happened in verse 35. Jesus went
from teaching *by* the water to teaching His disciples *in* the water. He
sent them out into the lake in a boat, where they quickly found themselves threatened by a furious storm. As I would have done, the disciples
panicked and rushed to wake up Jesus, who was peacefully asleep.

It's not that the storm wasn't real or dangerous or serious. It was.
But the real danger to the disciples was not the wind and waves; the real

danger was their lack of faith (v. 40) and confidence that Jesus was with them—faithful in the storm, able to get them through, and powerful enough to calm the chaos.

Jesus had to take His disciples from the lakeside to the lake to show His power, goodness, and faithfulness. The chaos of the storm and not the classroom of the lakeside would be their greatest learning moment.

Do you find yourself on a boat in the water in the middle of a storm? Do you need to be reminded that Jesus is God with you and for you, even in the middle of a storm?

Father, You are my help and my shield. My heart rejoices in You. I know that right now, with all my circumstances swirling around me, You are present. You are my God and my Savior, and I will trust in You. Increase my faith, and continue to show me Your faithfulness. In Jesus' name, amen.

- When has Jesus used the chaos of a storm instead of a classroom to increase your faith?
- How do storms reveal not only what you *do* believe but also what you *don't* believe?

....

....

....

....

....

....

11

Know Your Stuff

*Everything comes from you, and we have given
you only what comes from your hand.*

—1 CHRONICLES 29:14

J was beside myself with excitement one spring afternoon. Carrying my brand-new driver's license in my purse, I snagged the car keys from my dad and took the Cutlass for a spin—all by myself! It didn't matter that it was an old clunker, complete with rust spots and faded army-green paint. I was thrilled to call it "my car."

Maybe you experienced pride of ownership with your first bicycle. Or maybe, after years of scraping and saving, it was the joy of owning your very first home. Whether they're large or small, we like our things. But it begs the question, who really owns our stuff?

The Bible gives us a true perspective of what we call "ours."

In 1 Chronicles 29, we see King David preparing to build God's temple. He mentioned that he would spare no resource toward the construction. After gathering the resources for the temple, David praised the Lord, saying, "Praise be to you, LORD, the God of our father Israel, from everlasting to everlasting. Yours, LORD, is the greatness and the power and the glory and the majesty and the splendor, for everything in heaven and earth is yours" (vv. 10–11).

He continued: "But who am I, and who are my people, that we should be able to give as generously as this? Everything comes from you, and we have given you only what comes from your hand" (v. 14).

Wow. Did you catch that?

"Everything comes from you, and we have given you only what comes from your hand."

What an amazing perspective on our possessions. It's a subtle but crucial shift to realize that everything we work for here on earth really doesn't belong to us.

The question comes down to this: Who owns your stuff? Will you willingly share so others' lives may be bettered? The satisfaction from serving God in this way never rusts, tarnishes, or fades (1 Peter 1:4).

> Dear God, help me remember that You own all my stuff. Give me the
> same mind-set as King David, to share with others so Your work can
> be done and others' lives can be touched. In Jesus' name, amen.

❧ It's sometimes hard to see everything as the Lord's and not your own. In the space below, list some of the items that you have a hard time *not* seeing as yours. Ask God to help you hold these with open hands, and confess that they are blessings from Him meant for His glory.

....

....

....

....

12

The Security of Self-Control

Ruth

Like a city whose walls are broken through
is a person who lacks self-control.

—PROVERBS 25:28

*I*n the ancient world, cities were often protected by strong and sturdy walls. These walls surrounded the city, keeping those who lived there secure from outside threats. So having broken city walls put the people in a dangerous and vulnerable spot.

The writer of Proverbs used this familiar imagery to illustrate the importance of having and exercising self-control: "Like a city whose walls are broken through is a person who lacks self-control" (Proverbs 25:28). A city can have walls that are strong in one place but not in another. These holes or compromised sections of one part of the wall can leave us at risk. Just as strong walls were the secret to a strong and secure city, self-control is one important characteristic of a strong and secure person.

So what is self-control, and how can we experience more of the security it promises? It's helpful to think of self-control as a combination of our desires and our decisions. Self-control is a grace that God increasingly gives us as we abide in Christ and keep in step with His Spirit (Galatians 5:22–23). As we are being changed from the inside out, we should begin to experience a change in our desires. The Holy Spirit gives us new desires and longings that are set on honoring Christ.

But self-control is also making God-honoring decisions fueled by our changing desires. With renewed desires and decision making, we begin to live with greater wisdom. We are no longer slaves to whatever thought enters our minds. Our bodies don't have mastery over us. Sinful emotions don't take us captive.

Self-control is a gift of God's grace that guards you. Where are you lacking self-control? What parts of your "wall" are broken through? God wants to not only settle your soul but also secure it. Open your heart today to the work of His Spirit. Let Him fill you and fortify your life through His presence and power.

> Father, fill me with Your Spirit. Show me the broken walls in my life.
> Give me grace and wisdom. Cultivate in me the fruit of self-control.
> Take my thoughts, attitudes, longings, emotions, and members of my
> body and make them pleasing to You. In Jesus' name, amen.

- ❧ How have your "broken walls" been dangerous to you, your family, or those around you?
- ❧ What is one way you can begin to experience and exercise greater self-control?

....

....

....

....

13

Noticing Your Necessary People

Karen

God created human beings in his own image. In the image of
God he created them; male and female he created them.

—GENESIS 1:27 NLT

My two small children huddled together, giggling with glee. It wasn't Christmas or Easter. It was a different holiday—Mr. Brown Day.

Let me explain.

Mr. Brown was our mailman. But he delivered more than just bills and packages. He distributed smiles to those along his route. He was never too busy to chat with a lonely widow or ask a youngster about his Little League game.

We took the kids shopping for trinkets for Mr. Brown: a squirt gun for him to use to ward off the neighborhood dogs and a gift certificate to the local Dairy Queen so he could take Mrs. Brown out for a "fancy dinner." We baked cookies and poured lemonade into cups. Then we hid inside by our front door and waited with party blowers and confetti.

"Surprise!" we shouted as we threw open the door. "It's Mr. Brown, the best mailman in town! Today is officially Mr. Brown Day!"

To say he was surprised would be an understatement. He wanted to know what all the ruckus was about. My daughter told him we had been studying in the Bible about not just saying we love people but really showing them. Mr. Brown enjoyed the refreshments, gave each child a hug, and then went on his way with confetti still in his hair.

A week later he stood on my porch and said, "I have to tell you—I am *still* not over Mr. Brown Day." His voice cracking, he continued, "You know, I have been a mailman on this street for thirty-three years, and no one has ever done anything like what your family did for me. Thank you for Mr. Brown Day."

Noticing the people who provide necessary services in our lives shouldn't be an afterthought. We should show love to these necessary people because when we do, we acknowledge the fact that all humans are created in the image of God (Genesis 1:27).

Every day and every week, our lives naturally intersect with those of many people, all of whom bear God's image. Each person in their role demonstrates some aspect of God's character and His care for us. Our hairstylist cares for the very hairs on our head (Matthew 10:30). Our carpet cleaner can make our carpets as white as snow (Psalm 51:7). (Well, except for that one pesky grape juice stain.) Our medical professionals help us live, breathe, and have our being (Acts 17:28).

Yes, everywhere we look we see reflections of God's creative genius and His loving care in the people who serve us. Our lives can take on new meaning and be an exciting adventure if we stop to notice these necessary people.

Which "necessary person" will you bless today?

Father, thank You for the people You have placed in my life who serve me faithfully each week. When I see these image-bearers, may I also see You. In Jesus' name, amen.

❧ Write down at least one necessary person in your life and how you can bless him or her in the near future. Whether it's with confetti or another way of expressing heartfelt thanks, put something on your calendar so you don't forget to put action to this plan.

....

....

....

....

....

....

....

....

....

....

....

....

....

....

14

Why Are You So Angry?

Ruth

The LORD said to Cain, "Why are you angry?
Why is your face downcast?"

—GENESIS 4:6

The first sin recorded for us in the Bible outside of the garden of Eden is the sin of Cain killing his brother, Abel. We're told that Abel kept the flocks and Cain worked the soil (Genesis 4:2). In time, both men brought an offering to the Lord. While we're not told all the details, we learn that the Lord looked with favor on Abel's offering but not Cain's.

What was Cain's response? Genesis 4:5–6 tells us that he became angry. Then God asked the questions, "Why are you angry? Why is your face downcast?" Not only had Cain acted in anger by killing Abel, but his heart was being driven by a selfish or sinful desire that motivated his anger.

This is why learning to question our own angry thoughts, attitudes, and actions can help us overcome this dangerous emotion. Probing behind or underneath our anger helps us see the real reason we get angry.

Anger wears many hats. Sometimes it looks like punishing others with silence, withdrawal, explosive words, or emotional outbursts. Other times it looks like pouting and sulking. And in some cases, it looks like harsh and unrealistic demands.

Not all anger is bad or sinful. God gets angry, but His anger is always good, right, and justified. His anger is an expression of what He loves. But our anger is often sinful and self-seeking.

Sometimes anger reveals not what we want, but what we have and are afraid of losing. Maybe it's a sense of control, someone's approval, or security. Often times when what we value most is threatened, we act out in anger to prevent losing it.

Is your anger revealing something you are fearful of losing? What does your anger reveal that you treasure most? The next time you get angry, learn to ask, "Why?" Allow God to show you what is really driving your anger.

God wants to change us from the inside out. Not just our actions, but our hearts.

Father, show me the real cause of my anger. Through the work of Your Spirit, change me from the inside out. Root out selfish and sinful attitudes that are harmful to my relationships with others. Give me wisdom and understanding as I desire to be transformed into the likeness of Your Son. In Jesus' name, amen.

- As you think about your own life, how does anger express itself most often?
- How has the fear of losing something you treasure caused you to be angry?

....

....

....

15

When Loneliness Crushes Your Heart

Karen

The LORD appeared to us in the past, saying: "I have loved you with an everlasting love; I have drawn you with unfailing kindness."

—JEREMIAH 31:3

J will never forget the day of my senior prom. Not because I had a handsome date who swept me off my feet as we danced the night away—that wasn't the case. Not because I was able to purchase the perfect dress I'd always dreamed of wearing; I wasn't. Not even because I went with a group of girlfriends who all decided to go stag and then had a blast doing "the bump" on the dance floor together. (Hey, it was the mid-eighties, and "the bump" was all the rage!)

No, I remember the occasion vividly because it was the day I decorated the school gym, set up the food buffet, and then went home to spend the evening with the cast from *The Dukes of Hazzard* as my only companions.

I was on the prom committee that hung streamers and set out vases of fresh flowers to help make the evening magical. And because I worked at the restaurant chosen to cater the finger foods, I also carved a watermelon, filled it with fresh fruit, and brought it, along with platters of cheese and crackers and other assorted hors d'oeuvres, for the excited attendees to enjoy.

But there would be no prom night for me. I hadn't been asked to go. My senior year of high school wasn't really a time of fun and friends. It was a year full of sorrow and rejection, of many nights spent home all alone, feeling left out and unloved.

In elementary and middle school I seemed to have little trouble finding friends to call my own. But in the eighth grade, after repeating some gossip about a girl in my class, I lost a slew of friends. I was banished from the popular table at lunch and forced to find a new group of friends.

This smaller group of friends sufficed throughout my first half of high school. But then during the fall of my junior year, I turned my life over to Christ. This life-altering decision meant there were parties I would not attend and activities I simply had no interest in engaging in. My circle of friends grew smaller and smaller.

Mentally reliving this time brings back sadness, but it also reminds me that this was the exact season of life that catapulted me into the arms of Jesus.

Today's verse describes the deep love of God—unfailing, everlasting. Complete and thorough. With no signs of stopping.

Prom flowers wither. Cliques and schoolyard statuses soon go away. But we will never be found lacking when it comes to the love of our heavenly Father.

If you have a lonely and trampled heart, soothe it with the comfort of this mind-blowing truth: God loves you forever and will never leave you. The end.

Father, thank You for how You always welcome me and have never rejected me. Not only have You loved me in the past, but

You will love me forever. I am blessed to know Your steadfast,
perfect, unmatchable love. In Jesus' name, amen.

 споры In what part of your life do you most need to feel the everlasting
love and unfailing kindness of God?

....

....

....

....

....

....

....

....

....

....

....

....

....

....

....

16

Your True Identity

If anyone is in Christ, the new creation has come:
The old has gone, the new is here!

—2 CORINTHIANS 5:17

*I*t seems silly now, but I remember the feeling of seeing the title "assistant manager" next to my name for the first time. I was fresh out of college and ready to take on the world! My job wasn't terribly glamorous or high paying, but the new title and position gave me a sense of worth I found myself quite comfortable with. Unfortunately, as I would learn in the years to come, this is just one of many ways it is tempting to look to others, or other things, to find my identity.

What is it that really defines us and drives us? Who are we? Our identity is our sense of well-being, significance, or worth. Because all of us are looking for worth or identity, we inevitably end up creating our own identities. We may find an identity based on a job or career, as I first did. We base our worth on our social networks, our possessions, our successes, and even our failures.

The danger in looking to these areas to find identity is that they are not truly who we are. These identities are moving targets. They never last. They are only temporary. Even worse, when we look to anyone or anything other than who God says we are, we are really turning it into an idol. God our Father calls us into a new identity that never changes. Because it is rooted in what Jesus has done for us and what our Father thinks of us, it doesn't go away.

What does it mean to find our worth or identity in God? It means that we really are, like today's verse says, new creations. Because of our faith in Jesus, He now lives in us through the presence of the Holy Spirit. We are fully and completely loved. Accepted. Treasured. We are of incredible worth and significance not because of what we do but because we are made in God's image. There is such joy and freedom when we live out of the identity, acceptance, and approval we have because of Jesus.

Don't look to others to get what only God can give you! He alone loves you perfectly, and His love is sufficient to give you your true worth and identity.

> Father, I know You love me completely and unconditionally. Show me the
> areas where I am tempted to find my worth in the wrong places. Help me
> rest in and rely on the love You have for me. In Jesus' name, amen.

- In what ways are you most tempted to look to others for approval instead of looking to God?
- What is one way you can begin to root your identity in God's unchanging love?

....

....

....

....

17

The Point of All These People

Karen

"A new command I give you: Love one another. As I have loved you, so you must love one another. By this everyone will know that you are my disciples, if you love one another."

—JOHN 13:34–35

*E*ach day I witness a people parade. I'm sure you see one too. Whether in person, online, or on a screen, the people procession marches on.

You see your spouse, or maybe a roommate, first thing in the morning. Maybe a child crosses your path in need of a little breakfast. Your phone does a buzzing ballet on your kitchen counter alerting you to a friend's text message. A flowery card arrives in the mail from your grandma. Another swipe of your phone screen again reveals more relationships—from church, family, life.

What's the point of all these people in the parade?

Scripture says much about how we should and should not treat each other. In fact, the New Testament contains dozens of verses with relational instructions, all containing the telling phrase "one another."

Today's passage, John 13:34–35, showcases "one another" verses spoken by Jesus Himself. He is the model for love. His love is sacrificial. Consistent. Unconditional. Without strings attached.

Here's another "one another" verse we can apply to relationships with the people in our parades: "Be devoted to one another in love. Honor one another above yourselves" (Romans 12:10).

As we honor others, we reflect Jesus. We accurately model for others the love of Christ toward us when we seek to love others in the same way. If the Lord Himself put others first, then even though at times it is oh-so-challenging, we can strive to do so too!

We can forget that relationships aren't easy. I have to remind myself that they require loyalty and steadfast devotion. Sometimes marriages dissolve because feelings fade. We give up on friendships when they get hard. We decide our children have so severely disappointed us that we let our relationships with them dwindle as well. But the command in this portion of Romans is clear: don't hang up on your relationships; hang in there instead. (I am not speaking of damaging and abusive relationships, of course.)

If our perspective each day can be "I am in it for you" instead of "What is in it for me?" we'll discover the joy of serving Jesus without expecting anything in return.

Let's choose today to show a little "one another" living as we honor others and reflect the gospel of Jesus to all the people in our lives. Yes, even that person who rains on your people parade today.

> Father, help me look at my relationships with the people in my life as opportunities to show love and reflect the gospel. Give me strength not to grow weary. Help me honor others and love them with the love that You've shown me. In Jesus' name, amen.

❧ Find an additional "one another" verse from Scripture and write it below. What relational instruction does this verse give you?

18

Do Not Be Anxious

Ruth

Don't worry about anything; instead, pray about everything. Tell God what you need, and thank him for all he has done. Then you will experience God's peace, which exceeds anything we can understand. His peace will guard your hearts and minds as you live in Christ Jesus.

—PHILIPPIANS 4:6–7 NLT

We were supposed to be enjoying a family movie on Christmas night. It was the end of a long day full of family, food, and, of course, presents. But instead of having a leisurely night on the couch, we were rushing our oldest daughter to the emergency room because she was having difficulty breathing. And as the moments passed, the worry was suffocating me too.

My mind darted in about a hundred different directions. Doing my best to believe the words I was recalling, I began to pray Paul's words in Philippians 4:6: "Do not be anxious about anything, but in every situation," even on the way to the hospital, "present your requests to God."

Our daughter turned out to be just fine. Doctors checked her throat with a scope and didn't find anything, so we think she may have had a piece of food stuck in her throat that dislodged on the way to the hospital. Still, in the midst of the unknown, not worrying is easier said than done.

When anxiety is great within us, God invites us to bring the weight of what we are carrying to Him. He draws us near to let us know He is with us. Whether our anxiety is because of health, relationships, a job, finances, or friendships, God wants us to remember we are not alone.

I love the promise of today's verses. Not only do we bring our worry to Him, but God promises to guard our hearts and minds with peace. Paul uses the military term *guard* to illustrate that God's peace stands guard or protects us from excessive and unhealthy anxiety. What is this peace? It's not just a feeling, but the assurance of being right with God. The kind of peace Paul is talking about in these verses is a settled and anchored soul. It is a deep assurance that because of what Christ has done for us, all is well. God is with us and for us no matter what.

What are you anxious about today? Whatever situation you are in, take it to your Father, who loves you and is with you. May the peace of knowing Jesus, and being known by Him, guard your heart and mind. May His peace settle your soul today.

Father, I know You are with me. I bring all of my anxiety to You today. Give me faith where I am lacking. Help me trust You, knowing that You are in control. Guard my heart and my mind with Your peace. Stand guard for me so that I might experience the joy and hope of letting You carry my worry. In Jesus' name, amen.

∞ What are you most anxious about today?
∞ What is the connection between controlling your thoughts and experiencing God's peace?

....

....

....

19

Decisions, Decisions

Karen

"My command is this: Love each other as I have loved you. Greater love has no one than this: to lay down one's life for one's friends."

—JOHN 15:12–13

I have a confession. I love to get my way. Oh, I go about it rather cryptically, appearing to just be logical or thoughtful, but really, deep down inside, I know what I want. And usually I know just how to get it.

Perhaps this is one of the reasons why I love going to a coffeehouse. I can step up to the counter and rattle off to the barista my high-maintenance order, and my coffee turns out just as I want it.

While getting my way works at the coffeehouse, sometimes with the people closest to me, it gets in the way of my relationships.

From matters as small as what brand of ketchup to buy to huge decisions such as purchasing a house, I am very vocal and equally convincing about getting my way. And my large-and-in-charge bossy ways can cause conflict and friction with others.

This dilemma really isn't new. Our ancestor Eve exhibited this behavior back in the garden of Eden when she decided she knew better than God. She ate the fruit of the tree of the knowledge of good and evil, which God commanded her not to eat. Humankind's relationship with God experienced its first conflict, and sin entered the world.

To try to get our way, we might employ various tactics: reasoning, arguing, pleading, or even pouting—anything to secure the outcome we desire. But one day when reading today's passage, I gained a fresh insight into this familiar scripture.

I used to think of these verses in terms of the dramatic ways people might lay down their lives, like putting oneself in harm's way to save a friend from a deadly injury. Or a soldier might willingly give up his or her life on the battlefield. While these are certainly true and noble, I have come to think of this passage in more practical ways.

What if we gave up our quest to get our own way in everyday life? What if we stopped needing to be the one in our relationships who insists on all decisions going our way? This action of laying aside our desires for another's certainly is a way to show love.

It hasn't been easy, but viewing these verses as encouragement to stop trying to get my own way and let others decide has been so freeing! I have learned that others have good ideas and allowing someone else to choose helps me become less selfish. Yes, laying down our lives in even the smallest ways shows love for others and reverence for Christ. And it helps us decision-loving gals learn to let go and let others have a say. They might even thank us by buying us our favorite high-maintenance drink!

Father, forgive me for the times when I try to get my own way without listening to others or letting them in on the decision-making process. I want to learn to lay down my life—in ways both big and small. Help me be more like Your Son. In Jesus' name, amen.

In what areas of life do you like to get your way? In what ways could you show love to others by laying down your desires?

20

Letting Others In

Ruth

> *"I no longer call you servants, because a servant does not know his master's business. Instead, I have called you friends, for everything that I learned from my Father I have made known to you."*
>
> —JOHN 15:15

What does it mean to be a friend? It must have been no small thing for those first disciples to hear Jesus say, "I have called you friends" (John 15:15). Not servants. Not slaves. But friends. He had let them in to His life, and they let Him in.

By faith in Jesus, we not only increasingly begin to know God, but God intimately knows us. This is the heart of what it means to be in a relationship with God. It is an intimate friendship in which we give and receive.

But what about friendships with people? The friendship we have with God, through Jesus, lays the foundation for every other friendship. In Christ, we have full acceptance and love from the God who made us. It enables us to move toward others, helping us to love and serve those we are closest to.

But when it comes to letting others in, sometimes it's a different story. There is a big difference between being a good friend and allowing good friends in.

To create and cultivate deep friendships, we must be willing to be vulnerable. I'll be the first to admit that this isn't the easiest thing for me to do! A meaningful friendship requires that we share our joys and our struggles on a deeper level. It takes the willingness, in time, to let someone else know what is really going on. How they can pray for us. What we are struggling with. Ways they can love or support us. Vulnerability is like opening a window into our hearts, allowing a friend not only to know us more deeply but to love us more completely.

Sometimes our fear of being known keeps others out. Other times it's our pride. Maybe we tell ourselves we don't want to bother others with what we are going through. Regardless of the reason, all of these keep us from building the kind of friendships God desires for us.

Take a moment and think about your closest friendships. How can you take a step toward opening up more and letting others in?

> Father, I know You love me and accept me in Christ. Your love is
> unconditional. Help me move toward others in greater humility, love,
> and vulnerability. Teach me to open up and allow others to know me
> and love them with truth and grace. In Jesus' name, amen.

∞ What is your biggest obstacle to building deeper friendships?
∞ Why do you find it difficult to be vulnerable?

....

....

....

....

21

How to Hear a Heart-Drop

Karen

The hearts of the people cry out to the Lord.
—LAMENTATIONS 2:18

*I*t wasn't much to look at. It was a chunky hardcover children's book, its pages faded and well-worn. It had been gradually gathering dust and fingerprint smudges for nearly seventy-five years. Yet I was brimming with eagerness as I delicately wrapped my friend Trisha's present in pale aqua tissue paper.

Why was I so thrilled to give a used book to a friend? This gift was the response to a heart-drop. Let me explain.

Trisha and I were born the same year, so we had many common memories of being kids in the 1980s. Once while discussing our school days, Trisha mentioned how she'd seriously struggled with reading, but her face brightened as she recalled a small victory: "There was one book I actually could read cover to cover. It was called *Mary Lee and the Mystery of the Indian Beads*. I'd curl up on the sofa and read the whole thing. Oh, how I loved the feeling I got from reading that book!"

That story was more than just a window into Tricia's past. It was what I call a "heart-drop." A heart-drop is when a person, either directly or in a cryptic way, gives you a peek into his or her heart. It may be through actual words, or you might pick up on a feeling.

Trisha's heart surfaced that day as I recognized her longing for someone to say, "I'm listening. I hear you." I left our conversation determined to find a copy of that book. Thanks to an online site, I victoriously scored one.

When Trisha opened her gift that night in her living room, she looked up at me with such excitement. "How did you know?" she exclaimed. I reminded her of our conversation from months earlier, which she'd totally forgotten about.

Lamentations 2:18 was written during the time the ancient Israelites were held in captivity. The first part of the verse announced that God hears our heart cries: "The hearts of the people cry out to the Lord."

God knows what pains us and what brings us pleasure, but often He uses people to respond to the cries of others.

May we become skilled at tuning our ears to the heart-drops of those around us and then responding with a thoughtful gesture. It doesn't have to be an elaborate gift. It can be a kindly spoken word. A handwritten note. A loving text or an encouraging comment left on social media. A shared conversation over a cup of coffee. A brief moment when we put ourselves to the side for a moment to notice. To respond. To echo God's heart toward another.

Hearing a heart-drop is an art we must lovingly cultivate. It can lead to the most wonderful times of encouragement as we make it our habit to listen and to love.

Dear Father, may I learn to lean in and listen,
hearing the heart cries of others and then reaching
out in Your love. In Jesus' name, amen.

❧ Can you recall anyone who recently gave you a glimpse of her heart while talking? Is there any way you can respond to this invitation?

....

....

....

....

....

....

....

....

....

....

....

....

....

....

....

22

When God Closes a Door

Ruth

Paul and his companions traveled throughout the region of Phrygia and Galatia, having been kept by the Holy Spirit from preaching the word in the province of Asia. When they came to the border of Mysia, they tried to enter Bithynia, but the Spirit of Jesus would not allow them to.

—ACTS 16:6–7

I have always prided myself on the principle of "patience + persever-ance = success." I am not a quitter. And for most situations, there is wisdom in sticking it out and seeing something through.

But there is another principle in the Bible that I find myself wrestling with often. The God who calls us to patiently endure is also the God who closes doors. He is the One who redirects our plans, frustrates our efforts, and shows us there is something better if we would only trust Him.

It's comforting to know that even the apostles, those early followers of Jesus sent out to preach the good news, had a difficult time discerning and understanding God's will. A great example of this is found in Acts 16. Paul and his companions were setting out on another missionary journey to take the good news of God's love to new and different territo-ries. It was clearly an open door.

But soon after embarking on this journey, we're told in verses 6–7 that God closed some doors. The Holy Spirit kept them from traveling toward an opportunity in Asia and would not allow them to enter Bithynia either. We're not told what Paul's response was, but we can imagine he was likely confused, disappointed, or even discouraged. Yet several verses later, we see that God was opening a different door. There was a better opportunity. In God's wisdom and timing, He was redirecting Paul's plans.

Has God closed a door for you? Is there something you set out to do or accomplish that you are now beginning to sense may be a closed door? Don't be discouraged. Don't give up. As you continue to pray for God's wisdom and direction, remember that God is faithful to open a new door.

His plans and purposes always prevail. And when they do, we see that what He had in mind is always better!

> Father, I believe and trust that You are sovereign, in control, and directing my steps. Give me wisdom to see when to press on and when to humbly move in a new direction. Guard my heart from growing frustrated, and help me trust You even when Your plans are different from mine. In Jesus' name, amen.

- ∞ How do you know when to persevere and when to acknowledge a closed door?
- ∞ How have you seen God open a new door when He closes another door?

....

....

....

23

Why Chipped Crock-Pots Are Holy

Karen

Each of you should use whatever gift you have received to serve
others, as faithful stewards of God's grace in its various forms.

—1 PETER 4:10

*M*y Crock-Pot is a culinary eyesore. Oh, on the day it was purchased, it was a gorgeous and functional domestic tool—sleek and shiny, with a newfangled "keep warm" feature. But today this kitchen staple sits silently on my pantry shelf, nicked and chipped, practically tuckered out from nearly two decades of use.

Although I hate to admit it, at times I have succumbed to slow-cooker envy, especially when I spy some of the stunning new styles. Some are digital and programmable. Others have cute little clip-on signs to showcase what's simmering inside just waiting to delight everyone's taste buds. And then there sits my dilapidated model. Not pretty, but well-loved.

You see, my aging slow cooker has been an important ministry partner to me. It has housed batches of homemade three-alarm chili for the hungry football team. It has served vegetable soup to an exhausted mom who'd just welcomed home a newborn baby after a scary surgical delivery. It has contained savory beef stew that nourished the bodies of a grieving family we invited over to eat after the recent death of a loved one. Most often, it has warmed the tummies of my own family during an ordinary Sunday supper served on our old oak farm table.

I could grouse about the not-so-newness of my Crock-Pot, wishing for a newer model with all the bells and whistles—and sometimes I have. But as long as she's still chugging, I have determined to be grateful and not grumble. To just keep cooking. And inviting. And washing. And drying. And doing it all over again.

When we share our gifts, talents, and ordinary household items to bless and serve others, we aren't just being nice. We're being obedient to God's Word.

When we have a God-honoring perspective about our possessions and resources, our hearts and homes can become a wheelhouse for ministry. It's a perspective shift. We don't offer hospitality—or a home-cooked meal—to *impress* guests. Instead, we want to *refresh* them. Our aim is to use our homes as a ministry tool for building God's kingdom here on earth. To use our gifts to serve others, displaying God's grace as we do.

When we offer hospitality with gusto, without grumbling, complaining, or fretting over our not-so-nice-anymore stuff, we are doing exactly what pleases God—using our gifts for His glory.

A chipped and nicked Crock-Pot is a holy thing indeed.

> Father, may I make it my aim today to open both my heart
> and home without grumbling, using whatever gifts You have
> given me to serve others. In Jesus' name, amen.

❧ What household item do you possess that may not be in the finest condition? Have you used it for ministry in the past? How might you be able to glorify God by using it in the future?

24

Finding Strength in the Right Source

Ruth

> *Those who belong to Christ Jesus have crucified the*
> *flesh with its passions and desires. Since we live by*
> *the Spirit, let us keep in step with the Spirit.*
>
> —GALATIANS 5:24–25

aul gave us a clue about finding our strength in the right place in Galatians 5:24–25. We're told that because of our faith in Jesus, we now belong to Him. We have a new identity. God graciously gives us new desires and longings that are good and pleasing, leading to life instead of death. We "belong to Christ Jesus," and we no longer live life apart from God—in the "flesh."

Instead of trying to do life our way, on our own terms, following our own passions and desires, we are filled with God's Spirit. When we believe in Jesus, God puts His Spirit in us as a seal that we belong to Him (Ephesians 1:13). As we cooperate with the work of God's Spirit in us, we are changed, becoming more like Jesus as we abide in Him.

We are encouraged to remember that we now "live by the Spirit," and since we aren't doing life in our strength or wisdom, we are to "keep in step with the Spirit" (v. 25). Daily we are to confess the ways we resist God's work and help in our lives. We are to humbly ask the Holy Spirit to fill us, giving us the power and wisdom to accomplish all that is before us. After all, it is "'Not by might nor by power, but by my Spirit,' says the Lord Almighty" (Zechariah 4:6).

What are you trying to accomplish by your own might, power, or strength? What are you trying to do in your home, work, ministry, or community that is missing God's power and presence? He has promised to give us His strength. If we accomplish anything that truly matters for God, it will be in the strength He supplies through His Spirit.

Before you start your day today, rest and return to the right Source for drawing strength. I am confident you will find God sufficient!

> Father, thank You for the gift of Your Son on the cross, and
> for pouring out Your Spirit in my heart. Holy Spirit, fill me.
> Help me not to get ahead of You or lag behind, but always to
> keep in step with You. Give me strength. Help me draw from
> Your well that never runs dry. In Jesus' name, amen.

  ∾ What areas of your life are you pursuing in your own strength?
  ∾ What is one way you can begin to rely on the power and presence
    of the Holy Spirit in your life?

....

....

....

....

....

....

25

Coming Apart at the "Seems"

Karen

A heart at peace gives life to the body, but envy rots the bones.

—PROVERBS 14:30

J sat outside on our back deck, vigorously stirring my iced tea with a striped straw until the ice cubes formed a tiny whirlpool in my glass. But my midday beverage wasn't the only thing stirring. My emotions churned as well. See, I had been scrolling through social media posts on my phone.

Swipe after swipe made my heart sink further. I was already in a gloomy state from having dealt with a child's poor choice, a tension-filled dispute with my husband, and the too-tight jeans I wore that day, which at one time had been so loose on me that I'd almost donated them to the local thrift store.

Sigh.

As I scrolled through the highlight reel of images before me, all I could think was, *Gee, it must be nice. Everyone else seems to have it all together.* The scene played out a little something like this:

Swipe.

Wow. Seems like she has academically brilliant children.

Tap.

Man. Look at that fancy dinner with her smiling husband. They seem so happy.

Scroll.

Oh, lovely. A workout selfie at the gym. Seems like she has oodles of time to devote to exercise and a body and appetite that cooperate. Maybe I'll finally start my diet tomorrow. Or next Monday. Oh, who am I kidding? I'll never look like that.

And there you have it. A stroll down social media lane can leave us coming completely apart at the "seems." It always *seems* like everyone has it better than we do.

Today's key verse in Proverbs reflects this well: "A heart at peace gives life to the body, but envy rots the bones" (14:30).

Envy here doesn't just mean that initial, *Must be nice* thought. It means passionate and zealous jealousy.

The word *rots* means "decays." In this verse, that means the figurative death of one's very strength of life. But let's not just dwell on the dreary picture painted here. What about the other half of this verse?

The heart at peace literally means one that is sound, wholesome, healthy, and cured. So the way to have a healthy heart emotionally and spiritually is to keep envy at bay.

We do this by fighting against the "poor me" mentality. Thankfulness chases envy away and settles our souls in God's perfect peace. The next time we are tempted to come apart at the "seems" while staring at the pics on our phone, let's log off for a moment—or a week!—and start counting our many blessings.

May we be grateful to God for what we have and stop wanting someone else's life. Then we'll discover that true contentment isn't having what you want. It is wanting nothing more than what you already have.

Father, help me be earnestly grateful for all You've given me and stop wishing for someone's else's life. You are enough for me. In Jesus' name, amen.

❧ Whom or what do you envy? Write a prayer of confession below, and ask for help in changing this envy to thankfulness.

....

....

....

....

....

....

....

....

....

....

....

....

....

....

....

....

26

When God Seems Distant

Ruth

*How long, Lord? Will you forget me forever? How
long will you hide your face from me?*

—PSALM 13:1

When I slipped my arm around my dear friend, she melted in a puddle of tears. She felt like she was in the wilderness; it seemed God was not acting for her, and each month she waited for His answer became a heavier weight for her to carry. As we prayed together and cried together, she said, "It just seems like God is coming through for everyone else but me."

I won't pretend to fully understand what she was going through. Yet I couldn't help but wonder if what she was experiencing *was* God coming through for her. Just in a different way. In a harder way. Ultimately, though, perhaps it was in a way that was giving her what she needed most—deep transformation of her soul.

We've probably all felt forgotten by God at times. Each of our suffering is unique. The Bible is full of people who wrestled with painful questions and emotions, like today's verse: "How long, Lord? Will you forget me forever?" (Psalm 13:1). The psalmist gave words to our cries, longings, and questions. Sometimes it seems as if God is distant or that He is hiding His face from us.

Often in these times, He is doing something different, something deeper. Those unanswered prayers are not evidence of God's absence, but of God's unique activity in our souls. While we would all rather rush through painful seasons and circumstances, these are usually when God does some of His greatest work in us.

When God seems distant, He is teaching us to seek Him and desire Him for who He is more than what He can do for us. Many times He is cultivating in us a deeper intimacy, humility, perseverance, trust, and hope. The hard road is usually the holy road—the journey God uses to bring about the deepest change that our souls desperately need.

So if you are feeling as if God is distant, be encouraged that God is doing something deeper in you. He has promised never to leave you or forsake you (Hebrews 13:5). Don't rush this season. Don't try to fast-forward your circumstances. Lean into the God who loves you and is continuing to do a great work in you (Philippians 1:6).

Lord, I know things are not always the way they appear or feel. I trust You and invite You to continue shaping me, even when it seems You are distant. I know You desire to transform me and do something deeper in my soul. In Jesus' name, amen.

Where do you sense God wants to grow you the most in a difficult season or circumstance you may be facing or have faced in the past?

27

A Heavenly Relationship Recipe

Karen

*They sang a new song, saying: "You are worthy to take
the scroll and to open its seals, because you were slain,
and with your blood you purchased for God persons from
every tribe and language and people and nation."*

—REVELATION 5:9

For all but one year of my life I have lived in small towns within twenty miles of where I was born. These towns, though quaint and friendly, are not what you would call racially or ethnically diverse. Being raised in such an area presents challenges when it comes to getting to know people who look different from me.

Thankfully, my experience with a friend of my father's led me and my whole family to intentionally make efforts to know others who look, live, and worship differently than we do. This friend's name is Ray.

Ray was a coworker of my dad's who became very close to our family. He and I have completely different backgrounds and don't share the same race. But we do share similar hearts—hearts that love God, family, and ministry. Today Ray and I are like siblings, and he is even named in my father's will.

Currently, Brother Ray is the pastor of a church in the big city a few miles south of us. Years ago when his congregation purchased a larger church building and held their first service there, Ray invited my husband to be one of the guest speakers.

After the service, the church celebrated with a huge home-cooked dinner lovingly made by many of the women from that parish. My family and I were treated like royalty. We were seated at the head table and served the most delicious food, including many dishes I had never tried before. My children played in the nursery with the other children from the church. We exchanged hugs, well wishes, and recipes with many from the congregation.

It was an incredible experience, and what made it even more memorable was that we were the only family of our race in attendance for this celebration. It was good for our family—including our children—to be in the minority that Sunday.

Today's verse makes it clear that not everyone in heaven will look alike. There will be people from every tribe and nation and tongue. If heaven will be diverse, we need to make sure we are seeking out diversity while here on earth.

We must seek out new relationships. We must also resist using stereotypes when we encourage our children (and other young souls in our sphere of influence) to pursue diversity in their friendships.

Will you make it a point to purposely reach out to those who look and live differently than you? When you do, you reflect God's heart toward mankind while you also get a little glimpse of heaven. Why, you might just gain some new recipes in the process. But most of all, the recipe for love.

Father, I want to be intentional about getting to know and serving others who are different from me. Help me reflect Your love to them. In Jesus' name, amen.

❧ Does your circle of friends include only those who look and live like you do? What practical steps can you take to pursue diversity in your friendships?

....

....

....

....

....

....

....

....

....

....

....

....

....

....

....

....

28

Faith for This Place

Ruth

I said to you, "Do not be terrified; do not be afraid of them. The
Lord your God, who is going before you, will fight for you, as he
did for you in Egypt, before your very eyes, and in the wilderness.
There you saw how the Lord your God carried you, as a father
carries his son, all the way you went until you reached this place."

—DEUTERONOMY 1:29–31

*L*ife is full of joy, but it's also unpredictable and scary. We are in good company when we read the Bible—we find so many stories of God's people learning to trust Him and moving out in faith, even when fear is lurking close by. And we're encouraged that God has to keep reminding His people not to be afraid.

This is what I love about the Lord's reminder in Deuteronomy 1:29–31 to the Israelites before entering the land of promise. They too were afraid. They too were wondering, *What if God doesn't come through?* They too wrestled with trusting in God's goodness and faithfulness for the future, though they had seen it with their "very eyes" in the past (v. 30).

So just as He reminded the Israelites then, He reminds us now—*I am going before you. I will fight for you. You've seen Me do it before; I'll do it again.* Moses reminded them that the Lord had been good and faithful, carrying them like a father carries his son, all the way until they reached "this place" (v. 31).

Fear lives in the "next place." Fear lives in next week or next year. It lives down the road, when our kids are out of the house or when we grow old. It robs us of today. Causes us to be forgetful. Yet God wants us to remember that He has been faithful to provide all we need to get us to "this place." And if He has gotten us to this place, we can be sure He will get us to the next place, where He is present and sufficient.

What is making you fearful today? Are you resting in the place God has you, or are you anxious about where He is leading you? Fight fear today with the faith that God's presence and power are with you. May His peace, the peace that surpasses all understanding, guard your heart and mind from needless worry—because you know your God is near. And you know He is good.

> Father, thank You for Your faithfulness and goodness to get me to "this place." Give me hope today where my faith is weak. Guard my heart and mind with Your peace. Remind me that You are with me and for me, every step of the way. In Jesus' name, amen.

❧ In what ways do you live in the "next place" instead of in "this place"?

❧ How can you fight fear with faith today?

....

....

....

29

The Richest Poor Man in Texas

Karen

*Everything that was written in the past was written to teach
us, so that through the endurance taught in the Scriptures and
the encouragement they provide we might have hope.*

—ROMANS 15:4

The year was 1931—the height of the Depression era in the United States. In East Texas lived a man named F. K. Lathrop. Like many people at the time, Mr. Lathrop was a laborer struggling to stretch his meager weekly paycheck to provide for his family's needs. He worked at the local plow company earning a very small income. The ground underneath his feet was dry and hard—so hard, he had trouble even drilling for water.

But one ordinary day an attempt to drill revealed more than just H_2O flowing beneath this man's homestead. Mr. Lathrop found a secret that ensured his family would be provided for indefinitely. Hidden deep beneath the rocky soil was crude oil!

Soon the well was cranking out an astonishing thirty to forty thousand barrels of oil each day. Mr. Lathrop promptly sold the well for $3.5 million dollars, marched into his job, and quit. No longer did he have to squeak out a living. He was rolling in the dough—or, shall we say, swimming in the oil!

I find this Texas farmer's tale fascinating. For years he'd lived without knowing the secret his land was hiding—that he was the richest poor man in Texas! It wasn't until he drilled down deep that he discovered the black gold beneath the earth's crust. Although he lived as a struggling laborer, he was, in fact, a millionaire! But he was not able to live as a well-to-do mogul until he knew the truth of his situation and tapped into his wealth.

It's similar to how many of us live our lives today by never tapping into the wealth of Scripture.

Today's verse showcases the importance of God's Word in the life of believers. But the mere presence of a Bible at home—or its passages on a device's screen—doesn't ensure we'll experience all this verse promises. We need to drill down deep into Scripture and allow the truths of its Word to rush over our souls.

We can't just read the Bible; we need to allow the Bible to read us—convicting and changing us as it does.

Have you discovered the riches of digging deep into God's Word, or have you been squeaking out a mere existence, essentially living in biblical poverty?

Dust off your Bible. Take time to unearth the spiritual treasures it offers you there, buried beautifully in the words on its pages. When you know the truth of the living Word, you'll gain the confidence to boldly live out the truth in your life. This discovery—even greater than earthly riches—will change your life forever. It surely has mine.

Father, may I drill down deep into Your holy Word,
unlocking the truths of Scripture that will empower
me to live a godly life. In Jesus' name, amen.

❧ In what areas of your life are you reading God's Word, taking
in its knowledge, but not actually allowing it to change your
actions?

....

....

....

....

....

....

....

....

....

....

....

....

....

....

....

....

30

Grow Through It

Ruth

*We also glory in our sufferings, because we know that suffering
produces perseverance; perseverance, character; and character, hope.*

—ROMANS 5:3–4

All I wanted to do was get rid of my suffering. It was my fifth miscarriage, and I just wanted to fast-forward through the pain that was all too familiar to me. I didn't want to have to go through any of it! Looking back, though, I realize how much I would have missed that way. I wouldn't have missed the questions, the tears, or the longing for another child—I would have missed what God was doing in me.

The "glory" of suffering is lost if we try to just get through it instead of also growing through it. This is why throughout the New Testament we are called to suffer in the right way.

So what does suffering, done the right way, produce in us?

Romans 5:3–4 reminds us that God never wastes suffering. Painful seasons and circumstances are filled with meaning and purpose. They are indeed producing something in us. So as much as we love to escape suffering, God wants us to endure it. But not for just any reason.

We endure suffering and trials because we are confident God is working something in us, something deeper and far more transformational.

The apostle Paul said, "We also glory in our sufferings, because we know that suffering produces perseverance" (v. 3).

In the New Testament, to persevere is to remain focused on trusting and obeying God. Suffering or trials have a way of removing all the things that steal our focus from what matters most. Our pain purifies our priorities, bringing us back to greater love and loyalty. This is the kind of fruit suffering produces in us when we suffer the right way.

Are you in the middle of a painful season? Do you find it easier to want to escape suffering instead of enduring it? Whatever you are facing right now, don't rush it. Lean in to God. Listen to what He is really doing. Be patient in your affliction (Romans 12:12). God is doing something in you and for you. He wants you to grow through your suffering and not just get through your suffering.

Father, help me endure difficult circumstances with humility and trust. Teach me to slow down and grow in my suffering. I believe what You are doing in me is good. As painful as it may be, it is for my good. In Jesus' name, amen.

∞ How have you seen God do a good work in you from enduring suffering?

∞ What is one way you think God wants you to suffer well right now?

....

....

....

....

31

Find and Replace

Karen

Throw off your old sinful nature and your former way of life,
which is corrupted by lust and deception. Instead, let the
Spirit renew your thoughts and attitudes. Put on your new
nature, created to be like God—truly righteous and holy.

—EPHESIANS 4:22–24 NLT

I'm a big fan of a nifty editing tool on my computer called "Find and Replace." It allows me to locate an existing word and exchange it for one more suited to the meaning of my sentence.

At times I wish I had such a feature for my brain—a "Find and Replace" option that would help me keep my thoughts in a healthy place and in line with God's Word. Especially when it comes to setting my own agenda and getting my own way (better known as selfishness).

Even though I can't press a button and instantly swap out my old thoughts for new ones, I can still apply this "Find and Replace" process to my sometimes-selfish line of thinking.

When tempted to throw a pity party with only ourselves on the guest list (because, let's face it, no one fancies the company of a whiner), let's replace our negative notions with insight from God's Word.

Here are some "Find and Replace" examples. When we find ourselves

5

5

thinking one of the thoughts listed in bold, let's replace it with what God said in the verse that directly follows it.

If I don't look out for myself, who will?

"What is the price of five sparrows—two copper coins? Yet God does not forget a single one of them. And the very hairs on your head are all numbered. So don't be afraid; you are more valuable to God than a whole flock of sparrows" (Luke 12:6–7 NLT).

I'm entitled to my opinion.

"Don't repay evil for evil. Don't retaliate with insults when people insult you. Instead, pay them back with a blessing. That is what God has called you to do, and he will grant you his blessing. For the Scriptures say, 'If you want to enjoy life and see many happy days, keep your tongue from speaking evil and your lips from telling lies. Turn away from evil and do good. Search for peace, and work to maintain it'" (1 Peter 3:9–11 NLT).

I gotta look out for number one.

"Do nothing from selfish ambition or conceit, but in humility count others more significant than yourselves. Let each of you look not only to his own interests, but also to the interests of others. Have this mind among yourselves, which is yours in Christ Jesus" (Philippians 2:3–5 ESV).

But what about what I want?

"Carefully determine what pleases the Lord" (Ephesians 5:10 NLT).

How about it? Could your thought patterns benefit from some "Find and Replace" therapy? It is sure to center our minds on God and, as a result, make our relationship with Him, as well as with others, healthier, happier, and whole. Let's pursue an unselfish and God-pleasing attitude. Yes, let's make it our goal to find and replace.

Dear Lord, when I'm tempted by selfishness, may I align my thinking
with Your will and Your Word. In Jesus' name, amen.

❧ Think about any selfish thoughts you may be entertaining today.
(We all have them!) Next, write your own "Find and Replace"
example in the space provided, swapping that thought for a
scripture verse or two.

....

....

....

....

....

....

....

....

....

....

....

....

....

....

32

Nourishing Words

Ruth

The lips of the righteous nourish many.

—PROVERBS 10:21

There was once a monk who, like many followers of Jesus at the time, was looking for a deeper walk with God. This monk, Abbot Agatho, fled to the desert. The story goes that Abbot Agatho, aware of his temptation to sin with his words, carried a rock in his mouth for three years! He did so until he learned to be silent—or to control his lips.

I'm not ready to carry a rock in my mouth as a reminder to watch my words, but I am very aware of my own temptation to use my words unwisely. Because we serve a God who speaks and uses His words to bring life, we are reminded that our words really do matter. They matter in our marriage, our family, the workplace, our relationships, and our church. Our words really are an overflow of what is going on in our hearts (Luke 6:45), and they have the power to shape the hearts of those whom God has surrounded us with.

In Proverb 10:21, the writer said, "The lips of the righteous nourish many." With our words, we bring life, health, and good things to those we encounter. We make others better by what rolls off our tongue. With our lips, we are to avoid gossip, slander, malice, and idle talk, which steal life instead of nourishing it.

We can nourish those around us with words of encouragement. Speaking truth in love. Sharing our appreciation. Building others up with the truth and promises of God's Word. We nourish others when we speak with gentleness and compassion. We bring life when we choose not to speak words that could easily be used as weapons.

How are you using your words? Do your words bring nourishment to those around you? Take a moment and prayerfully consider how your words are bringing life or death to those you are closest to. Let's pursue the righteousness described in Proverbs—being one who uses her words to nourish not just some, but many!

> Lord, You are a God who speaks. As I reflect who You are to those around me, help me use my words wisely. Give me grace to "nourish many" with my lips. I confess that my words are not always used in a way that honors You. Forgive me and teach me to love and serve those around me with the words You give me. In Jesus' name, amen.

- ❧ Where do you struggle with your words the most?
- ❧ What is one way you can begin nourishing others with your words today?

....

....

....

....

....

33

Wait Training

Karen

They who wait for the LORD shall renew their strength;
they shall mount up with wings like eagles; they shall run
and not be weary; they shall walk and not faint.

—ISAIAH 40:31 ESV

Ever feel like God signed you up for an intense "wait-training" class? You pray. You ask. You anticipate God's answer, but like an internet page taking a long time to load, you must wait. And wait some more.

This waiting is no fun at all.

But just as physical weight training builds strength, so does spiritual wait training. We are promised this in today's verse.

How can waiting renew our strength? After all, doesn't waiting seem to sap our strength as we worry and fret and drum our fingers impatiently? It's exhausting playing the what-if game in our minds: *What if this doesn't work out? What if God's answer is no? What if the thing I fear the most actually happens . . . what then?*

All this worry-laden waiting can drain us rather than strengthen us. How can we turn this around and actually find ourselves renewed?

In the waiting times I have found that shifting my perspective replenishes my strength. I try not to think about those times of seeming silence from God as my sitting and anxiously anticipating a response.

But rather, I try to think of myself waiting as if I were a butler, maid, or restaurant server.

Those who "wait for the LORD"—as in serve Him, cater to Him, help Him accomplish His work, those who take His order and bring Him what He wants—they are the ones who renew their strength (Isaiah 40:31 ESV). They mount up with wings like eagles. They walk and do not faint.

As we serve, we become more aware of what the One we are waiting on desires. We become alert, attentive, and in tune with His wishes. We begin to take our eyes off of our problems and fix them on the Lord instead. As we do, we get a glimpse into His heart.

Even in those long, hard times of waiting for an answer, we continue to serve Him. Then, instead of the wait sapping our spiritual strength, the wait renews it as we seek to do the Lord's will.

Will you sign up with me for wait training? You'll grow stronger spiritual muscles if you do. But we must commit to this perspective: we won't just "wait for the LORD"; we'll wait on Him.

> Dear Lord, teach me to shift my perspective during those times
> of waiting and doubt. May I stop fretting and worrying and busy
> myself by serving You instead. In Jesus' name, amen.

∞ Write down a few things you are waiting for. How can you serve God while waiting on Him instead of fretting?

....

....

....

34

Creating Space for One Another

Ruth

Offer hospitality to one another without grumbling.

—1 PETER 4:9

When my husband and I were first married, we lived in a turn-of-the-century home that was built around 1903. One day as we sat on our front porch, looking down the street one way and then the other, it occurred to us that our street was lined with similar homes, all with cozy front porches. But it didn't take long for us to notice something else. No one was using them, or at least very few were.

For the most part, we live in a fast-paced, busy, and private culture. Depending on the neighborhood, we have to go out of our way to get to know those who live near us. Our front porches have largely been replaced by decks we build on the backs of our houses, giving us greater privacy and insulation from others.

But the Bible gives us a simple solution for loving and serving others well. It's a practice we don't see or experience very often anymore. Yet it has the power to show the love of Christ to others in a very tangible way. It is the practice of hospitality.

In the New Testament, hospitality is routinely encouraged (Romans 12:13). We are to love and serve others by opening our home and sharing a meal without grumbling (1 Peter 4:9). In fact, according to 1 Timothy

3:2, someone should not be a church leader without regularly practicing hospitality. And when we look at the Jesus' life, we discover that much of His ministry was around a table.

Hospitality is so much more than inviting someone over. It is an invitation to build a deeper and more meaningful friendship with a friend, coworker, or neighbor. When you open your home to someone, you are opening your heart to them. It is an invitation to know you and to be known by you. The simple act of opening your home to share a meal or a cup of coffee opens a door to others' hearts.

How might you use your home, a meal, or even just a cup of coffee to open your heart to someone else? A simple and ordinary invitation can be a powerful way to love and serve others the way Jesus did. Open your home and your heart, and just watch what God can do!

> Father, I believe the practice of offering hospitality is a picture of
> what You have done for me in Christ. You have invited me to know You
> and to be loved by You. Show me the power of offering my home and
> heart to others. Use the simple act of sharing time and food together
> to deepen friendships with others. In Jesus' name, amen.

- ❧ What is the difference between entertaining others and offering hospitality?
- ❧ What is one thing you can intentionally do to begin practicing hospitality?

....

....

....

35

Father Knows Best

Karen

*The Lord said, "It is because they have forsaken my law, which I
set before them; they have not obeyed me or followed my law."*

—JEREMIAH 9:13

The car was packed; the gas tank full; a cooler stood chock-full of sandwiches for the long ride. My three kids and I were gleefully off on a summertime adventure. In the midst of a stressful and busy move, we threw caution to the wind and took my friend up on an invitation to join her at a beachfront home she was being allowed to use for free.

Now, this was no small undertaking. It was going to be a seventeen-hour trip with three kids in the car.

We didn't have GPS back then, but I did use an online site that spit out detailed directions. I thought these directions would make the trip a piece of cake. So I printed them off, tucked them in a folder, and revved up the car's engine.

Before I left, however, my father called me. He spends winters near the beach where we were going. He offered to give me verbal directions since he has traveled that route twice a year for the past eighteen years and is very familiar with how to get there.

I reluctantly wrote down my dad's instructions. Then I tossed his directions into the glove compartment. I thanked him for the gesture but assured him I probably wouldn't need them. As I left, he said, "You might. Remember, father knows best!"

About halfway to our destination, I noticed that the exit number and the exit name on the internet's directions didn't match up. I chose to follow the exit number. Soon after that, I became completely lost. I got off the exit, headed back to where I'd made the turn, and tried again.

But this way didn't work either! When I got off again, I popped into a gas station and asked for help. The attendant smiled and handed me a piece of paper with corrected directions already written on it. Every day the gas station had dozens of lost travelers wandering into their establishment longing to get back on the right track.

Worried that the rest of my internet directions might be wrong as well, I quickly fumbled through the glove compartment to find my father's detailed instructions. I ran them by the gas station attendant. "Perfect!" he commented. "Just stick to your father's instructions and you won't be lost."

Like so much of life, we hear of newfangled shortcuts, ways to find happiness, or even new paths for getting to heaven. We must resist the desire to trust these so-called new ways and instead follow our Father's original instructions: the Holy Bible.

God's instructions are never wrong. They lead to peace, contentment, and a home with Him in heaven forever. Much better than a week at the beach!

Dear Lord, help me get and stay forever grounded in Your ancient instructions, the Bible. May I follow only Your holy ways. In Jesus' name, amen.

❧ Have you ever been in a situation where you got lost? How did you find your way out? What lesson did you learn?

....

....

....

....

....

....

....

....

....

....

....

....

....

....

....

....

36

Satisfying Our Deepest Hunger

Ruth

"Blessed are those who hunger and thirst for
righteousness, for they shall be satisfied."
—MATTHEW 5:6 ESV

oney, look at this omelet!" I said to my husband. We were on our way to one of our favorite restaurants in Ann Arbor, Michigan, and I was already looking at pictures of food from another local restaurant's Instagram page. "It's local farm to table. Organic. We *need* to try this place next!"

My husband was not fazed by my food enthusiasm. He knows me well enough by now to know I love all things food. He often jokes that I could work for the city, telling visitors where to eat. He's probably right! I love good food, and it seems like God does too.

Think about the way God wired us. The average human being has around ten thousand taste buds. Our taste buds have microscopic hairs that send messages to the brain telling us if something is sweet, salty, bitter, or sour. Food is far more than fuel. It is something to be enjoyed. Food is good and tasty, filling us with delight. No wonder we love to eat so much!

But the Bible reminds us about another side of food. Food is really only a pointer, directing us to what our souls crave most—joy and comfort and satisfaction in God. The Bible uses the language of food and drink often. Jesus said, "Blessed are those who hunger and thirst for righteousness, for they will be filled" (Matthew 5:6). The psalmist longed for God as he longed for water in a dry and weary land (Psalm 63:1).

As good and tasty as food is, it is meant to remind us not just what our stomachs need, but what our souls need—to be satisfied in Christ. He alone is the Bread of Life whose words sustain and strengthen us. He is Living Water, quenching our deepest thirst.

Like anything good, food can become a substitute for God. We can turn to eating or drinking to find the comfort, joy, or satisfaction that only God can bring. Food is essential. It is good. But in those moments when we are tempted to turn to food for comfort or satisfaction, remember that God wants to do far more than just feed our stomachs. He wants to fuel our souls.

Lord, You are my soul's desire. I long to know You more, experiencing the depths of Your love for me. Remind me each time I eat that my deepest longing is for fuel for my soul and not just food for my stomach. Only You can satisfy me. In Jesus' name, amen.

❧ How are you being controlled by your appetite instead of controlling your appetite?
❧ In what ways and in what situations does your soul crave God?

....

....

....

37

Answer Envy

Karen

"Call to me and I will answer you and tell you great
and unsearchable things you do not know."

—JEREMIAH 33:3

Do you ever envy God's answers to someone else's prayers? I remember almost choking on the words, "I am so happy for you!" in response to the breaking news that friends of ours from North Carolina had sold their house after it had been on the market for only twenty days.

To our friends, it had been a long twenty days. Houses were normally snatched up quickly in their area. During that time in our shaky Michigan economy, however, it took a bit longer for us. In fact, on the day they announced that their home now had a Sold sign in the front yard, my husband and I turned another page on our calendar, marking how long our house had been for sale—not twenty days, but twenty months, to be exact.

Although I was genuinely thrilled for my friend, I was also a tad green with jealousy.

I call this *answer envy*. It is that "poor me" mentality that creeps into my heart when God answers someone else's prayers more quickly than mine. Or when He responds to them with a "yes" but His answer seems to be a "no" for me, or at least a "not right now."

Over the years I have discovered that the cure for answer envy is not always easy because I must play an active role in my own healing.

What I need is a shift in perspective. When I call to God as encouraged in today's key verse, I must trust that He will keep His word. He *will* tell me "great and unsearchable things" that I do not know. Sometimes those things are the answers to my requests. But do you know what those great and unsearchable things more often are? They are the reasons He seems *not* to be answering my original request!

So instead of only begging God to "sell my house" or "take away my pain" or "fix my kid," I need also to ask myself some questions. Questions like, *What is my Creator trying to teach me that I might never learn if He were to suddenly pluck me out of this situation?* Or, *What character qualities is He trying to grow in me?*

Not available in quick microwave form, the cure for answer envy must be cultivated moment by moment.

We must believe that God will answer. He will clearly say yes, no, or not right now. He is able, ready, and willing to answer our prayers—here is the catch—*as He sees fit* and to grow us to be more like His Son in the process.

It took two years until our For Sale sign was finally replaced with a Sold banner. It was a long stay in God's waiting room. But I now know this to be true: I must not merely seek the answer to my prayer. Instead, I must seek a deeper relationship with the answer Giver.

> Dear Lord, thank You for Your perfect plans, Your perfect
> timing, and Your perfect way. In Jesus' name, amen.

  ❧ Are you currently experiencing "answer envy"? Answer this
question from today's devotion: *What is my Creator trying to teach*

me that I might never learn if He were to suddenly pluck me out of this situation?

....

....

....

....

....

....

....

....

....

....

....

....

....

....

....

....

38

Discovering Meaning in Work

Ruth

God saw all that he had made, and it was very good. And there
was evening, and there was morning—the sixth day.

—GENESIS 1:31

*I*f you have ever struggled to find joy and meaning in your work, you are not alone! Some estimate that over 75 percent of people are unhappy doing what they do. Let's be honest, sometimes it's easier to grumble our way through a workday or week. But is this really God's vision for work? What if God has more for us in the workplace? What about as a student, mom, ministry leader, or volunteer?

The opening chapters of the Bible record God in the act of work. Genesis 1 and 2 describe the act of God creating the world as *working*. He is busy. Active. Productive. Creative. Shaping. Forming. Producing. And if that is not enough, Genesis 1:31 tells us that God takes great joy in His work. We don't find Him complaining about all He has to do or grumbling about the inconvenience of disorder and chaos! He actually takes great delight in working. There is something inherently good and important and meaningful about work because God works.

The Bible doesn't stop there. We're told that not only does God work, but He has created us to work. In fact, work existed before sin entered the world. Work was a part of God's original and good creation. Genesis

1:26 tells us that we are made in God's "image" and "likeness." Because God works, we work. Work, no matter what we do for a living, can be an act of worship.

Work doesn't just exist for us. God desires that we become fully engaged and give ourselves to the calling of loving Him and others through our work. It's not just an opportunity to acquire possessions or self-worth. Ultimately work is an opportunity to serve God and serve others with the gifts, resources, and energy God has given us.

Do you need the reminder that work really is full of meaning and purpose? Every act, every task, no matter how small or seemingly unimportant, matters to God. And your work can be an act of worship to the God who works in you and through you.

Father, You are the King of creation. You are active, fully at work in Your good creation. Teach me to see all I do as an act of worship to You. Remind me of the great value and purpose of my work. Let my work be an avenue to love You and serve others. In Jesus' name, amen.

- How would you describe your attitude or understanding of work?
- In what way can your work become an act of worship?

....

....

....

....

....

39

Can You Pack a Lunch?

Karen

Another of his disciples, Andrew, Simon Peter's brother, spoke up, "Here is a boy with five small barley loaves and two small fish, but how far will they go among so many?"

—JOHN 6:8–9

*C*an a simple sack lunch change the world?

The scene was a mountainside, near the shore of the Sea of Galilee. Jesus was in the midst of a busy season of ministry. All around the crowds pressed in, hoping to capture a glimpse of Jesus.

We pick up the scene in John 6:5–7. "When Jesus looked up and saw a great crowd coming toward him, he said to Philip, 'Where shall we buy bread for these people to eat?' He asked this only to test him, for he already had in mind what he was going to do. Philip answered him, 'It would take more than half a year's wages to buy enough bread for each one to have a bite!'"

Not only had a crowd gathered, but it was a hungry horde. And they expected Jesus to feed them. Philip quickly began to crunch the numbers and determined just how impossible a little impromptu mountainside picnic would be. But what seemed an impossible feat to Philip would soon become a glorious display of God's power.

Another disciple, Andrew, piped up. He told Jesus that a young boy had five barley baguettes and two tiny fish. Not much of a lunch, but it was more than enough for Jesus.

This familiar story from Scripture often focuses on the young lad sharing what he had. But have you ever stopped to wonder where this child got the food? Had he been running an errand for his family, buying fish and bread at the marketplace as many Bible scholars surmise? Or maybe, as I heard a pastor once suggest, this was his own sustenance for the day—a sack lunch of sorts his mother had lovingly packed.

This child wasn't just armed with the food Jesus needed to nourish others; he also possessed a humble heart and a generous spirit. And he was best positioned to give because someone empowered him to do so. Yes, maybe his mama not only packed him a sack lunch, but she taught him some good manners as well. In the end, it resulted in many being nourished.

Many people could use your help. Whether you decide to give to a particular missionary or homeless shelter, whether you give financially or with your time, there are others out there who need you. These people are waiting for someone to help them so they can then go help others. But before these souls can do this, they first need to be filled up. They need their spiritual sack lunch packed.

Helping others soul be fed spiritually—by praying for them, encouraging them with scripture, or studying the Bible with them—not only changes their lives . . . it can help change yours as well.

Father, I want to generously give to others so they, in turn,
might change their worlds. In Jesus' name, amen.

How is God calling you to help nourish someone else spiritually?

....

....

....

....

....

....

....

....

....

....

....

....

....

....

....

....

....

....

40

Resisting the Urge to Defend Yourself

Ruth

Be careful to live properly among your unbelieving neighbors. Then even if they accuse you of doing wrong, they will see your honorable behavior, and they will give honor to God when he judges the world.

—1 PETER 2:12 NLT

Our family was in the process of transitioning from a church where my husband had served as a pastor. Change, anywhere, is difficult. So on one hand we understood the mixture of emotion many people felt. But what we were unprepared for was the amount of people talking about the transition in ways that were not entirely accurate.

We've probably all experienced the sting of people's comments. Live long enough and we inevitably have people who love us, are indifferent to us, and of course, just don't like us! But what do you do when people insult you or even say things that aren't entirely true of you? The Bible has a surprising answer: let your life be your greatest argument.

Of course, there is a time to lovingly and gently approach someone who has wronged you or misspoken about you. We are to humbly seek peace when it is possible. But there are certainly times when we have to resist the urge to get even, demand justice, or even defend ourselves.

In 1 Peter 2:12, Peter used Jesus as the best example of someone who suffered unjustly. Peter reminded us that our greatest defense is our lives. "Live such good lives" that even when people falsely accuse us, they may in time be won over because of our actions—the testimony of our lives. Peter told us that Jesus didn't try to get even. He didn't sulk, grow bitter, or vengeful. Instead, "He entrusted himself to him who judges justly" (v. 23). Jesus placed His life in God the Father's hands, knowing He alone is the One who judges completely, accurately, and with justice.

People's approval will come and go. But if we are in Christ, God's approval of us never changes.

Don't be moved by the approval or disapproval of people. You don't have to defend yourself. You have a Father who loves you and knows the whole truth about you. Let your life be your greatest argument!

> Father, thank You for loving me and accepting me in Christ. Remind me that Your approval never changes. Help me resist the urge to defend myself. I entrust myself to You, the One who judges justly. I know You fight for me, and in the end, Your approval matters most. In Jesus' name, amen.

∞ When is it appropriate to defend yourself?

∞ Why is it so important to "entrust" your life to the One who judges justly?

....

....

....

....

....

41

Answering Our Own Prayers

Karen

Jesus was praying in a certain place, and when he
finished, one of his disciples said to him, "Lord, teach
us to pray, as John taught his disciples."

—LUKE 11:1 ESV

A group of teenagers and I sat cross-legged on the church lawn, soaking in the warm summer sunshine. One of the girls had just returned from a mission trip in a developing nation, and I couldn't wait to hear about her experience.

"So, Renee, tell us about your trip," I inquired. "What is the one thing you think you will remember the most?"

I imagined her answer would have something to do with a child who captured her heart with a sweet smile. Or a church service she attended that was so very different from ours. Neither of these guesses was right.

"Oh, that's easy," Renee replied. "I will always remember it was on this trip when I learned how easy it is in our culture to answer our own prayers." Her statement stunned me for a moment. But before I could pipe up and ask her to explain further, she continued.

"You see, here in America, we bow our heads and say grace and ask God to 'give us this day our daily bread.' And then? We hop in our cars, run down to the grocery store, and buy a loaf or two. We ask Him to keep us safe and warm. Then parents buy their kids the best car seats available, and we crank up the furnace whenever we feel chilly. It is so easy in our culture to provide the answer to our own prayers. But the people I met on the trip? They pray God will give them their daily bread, not knowing if they will have enough food to feed their families that night. They ask God for things they can't always provide for themselves."

I had never thought of this concept before, and it caused me to think about two things.

First, I want to use my abundance to help answer someone else's prayers.

Second, I need to learn to pray bold prayers, asking God for the things that only He can bring about. That is, *if* they are in accordance with His will.

Today's key verse from Luke 11 gives me hope that I'm not alone in thinking my prayer life could use a makeover. Luke 11:1 reminds me that even the disciples wanted help learning how to pray.

My little chat with this spiritually sensitive teen changed me. I began to work into my prayers not only requests that God would help me be attentive to those who need my help, but also that He would help me make bold requests I can't possibly answer myself—and then that I would stand back in faith and watch Him work.

How about you? Is your prayer list full of items you can cross off yourself? Perhaps it's time you too began to ask, "Lord, teach me to pray."

Father, teach me to pray more boldly. Help me pray more
confident prayers that can't be answered on my own and can
only happen through Your power. In Jesus' name, amen.

What is a bold prayer you've been too uncomfortable to pray because the answer would take the supernatural power of God?

42

He Bends Down

Ruth

*Turn your ear to me, come quickly to my rescue; be my
rock of refuge, a strong fortress to save me.*

—PSALM 31:2

As I sat waiting for a friend to join me at a local coffee shop, I overheard part of a conversation from a woman who was visibly frustrated. She was a young woman, most likely in her late twenties or early thirties. A working professional. She was describing a meeting with her supervisor who for nearly twenty minutes never looked up from his phone as he answered questions, clearly multitasking and half listening.

I can see why she was so upset! Who wants to be half listened to? We've probably all done the same, in varying degrees. We try to do too much all at once. We half listen to a coworker, friend, husband, or even our kids. We are sort of there, or there just enough, but far from fully present.

While we have all been on both the giving and receiving end of this type of listening, one thing we can be confident of is that God does not listen to us this way. He is never distracted or annoyed. He is fully engaged, fully attentive, and faithful to respond.

The psalmist gave us a beautiful description of just how much God loves us and desires to listen to us. He wrote, "Turn your ear to me, come quickly to my rescue; be my rock of refuge, a strong fortress to save me" (Psalm 31:2). It's staggering to think about how the word translated as "turn your ear" can also be translated as "bow down your ear."

Imagine the King of kings, the Lord of all creation, the One we bow down to bending His ear to us. He doesn't listen from afar. He bends down, gets close, turns His ear to hear us. He is intimate, compassionate, and faithful to respond according to His will.

God loves us by listening to us. Even when He seems distant, He is not. He is present, faithful, and working out His purposes and promises, often in ways we can't see.

So cry out to Him. Don't stop seeking Him. In faith and persistence, draw near to the God who loves you by listening to you.

> Father, I know You ask me to come to You in faith and with persistence.
> Remind me of the way You are present, active, and compassionate toward
> me. Thank You for loving me by listening to me. In Jesus' name, amen.

&ptimes; How have you seen God work in your midst when you take time
to listen to Him?

&ptimes; What is most encouraging about the image of God bowing down
His ear to listen to you?

....

....

....

....

43

How to Have a Crack-Proof Spirit

Karen

*Because so many people were coming and going that they did
not even have a chance to eat, he said to them, "Come with
me by yourselves to a quiet place and get some rest."*

—MARK 6:31

I want honey in my tea! And a lemon slice too! Oh, and can I use
Great-Grandma's teacup, pretty please? I'll be careful," my then
five-year-old daughter sweetly asked as we were enjoying our afternoon
mother-daughter ritual.

Each day while her two baby brothers napped, we pulled out teacups
and saucers from my china collection and sipped herbal tea while I read
a book out loud to her.

That afternoon she was asking for permission to use an heirloom
piece that had been passed down through four generations in my mother's family. While I knew my little girl would be careful with the antique
pink-and-white china cradled in her little hands, something else made
me deny her request. I tried explaining it to her.

"Sweetheart, I know you'll be careful, but we can't have hot tea in
that cup. It has cracks. See?"

I showed her a few hairline fractures on the side near the handle. It wasn't cracked all the way through and could actually still hold water without leaking. However, if hot liquid were to be poured into it, the crack would give way, causing the cup to shatter.

There was just no way for the fractured piece to withstand the stress of a steaming beverage.

Our emotional lives are much the same. When we don't allow time to rest and regroup from the stresses of life, we allow cracks in our spirit that make us emotionally and spiritually fragile. We keep going at breakneck speeds, rarely slowing down long enough to be refreshed.

Mark 6:31 highlights the fact that even Jesus Himself found it important to get away for a while, to slow down and cease activity. Jesus urged His disciples to get to a quiet place. In doing so, they would find rest. Being alone and quiet with Him would restore their weary spirits.

In our fast-paced society, we are rarely intentional about creating a quiet place and spending time resting. As a result, stress chisels away at us, creating tiny cracks that, although barely visible, could cause us to shatter under the go-go-go pressures of everyday life.

Let's intentionally take time to slow down, get away, and rest.

If we make time to answer Jesus' call to go away with Him to a quiet place, we can crack-proof our spirits, making them strong and rendering us ready to handle life. A few quiet moments spent with Him can help make us strong enough to fulfill God's assignments for us in this season of life.

> Dear Lord, help me intentionally carve out time to reconnect
> with You in a quiet spot. I know You are waiting. I want to seek
> Your face and find true rest. In Jesus' name, amen.

❧ Can you see any stress fractures in your life? Where can you
carve space into your schedule for slowing down?

....

....

....

....

....

....

....

....

....

....

....

....

....

....

....

....

44

A Sneaky Form of Pride

God opposes the proud but gives grace to the humble.
—1 PETER 5:5 ESV

Peter didn't mince his words. He told it like it is. Probably because he knew so well the danger of pride. After all, he was always the first disciple to put his foot in his mouth! So when Peter, who was much older, wrote on the topic of pride and humility, he put it pretty plainly.

"God opposes the proud" (1 Peter 5:5 ESV).

God is not indifferent to our feeble attempts to steal the glory that only He deserves! He stands against it. He wants something different. Something better for us. And He promises to give grace to the humble instead. What makes pride such a serious issue to God?

For starters, it tries to elevate us *above* God, not just *away* from God. It puts us at the center. In our preoccupation with self, we are often quick to defend ourselves and puff ourselves up. But pride can also be competitive, always trying to get more or get ahead of others.

We often think of prideful people as those who love themselves. But did you know there is another sneaky form of pride? It can also show up in our hearts when we are always down on ourselves. Self-importance and self-loathing are two sides of the same prideful coin!

When we are always putting ourselves down, talking about how bad we have it, throwing pity parties, and fishing for reassurance or affirmation by making fun of ourselves, we still have *us* at the center.

Pride doesn't settle our souls, but humility can. The humble heart is one fixed on loving God and loving others. Humility thinks more about others and less about self. This is, after all, how Jesus loved us.

Today ask God to take your focus off yourself. Ask Him to give you the grace you need to love others more and keep a humble heart.

Father, You alone deserve to be at the center. Teach me to focus less on myself and more on others. Create in me a heart that is neither self-important nor self-loathing. Help me move toward others in the same way You have moved toward me—in love, grace, and humility. In Jesus' name, amen.

ॐ How does self-loathing most often show up in your life?

ॐ What is one way you can begin to "clothe yourself with humility" (1 Peter 5:5)?

....

....

....

....

....

....

....

....

45

Everybody's Got Somethin'

Karen

*Good sense makes one slow to anger, and it
is his glory to overlook an offense.*

—PROVERBS 19:11 ESV

My intense irritation at my husband's actions didn't show visibly. Since his mother was sitting behind us in the backseat of our car, I was careful to remain calm. However, I did sneak a darting glance toward him—a dagger that accurately conveyed how very much I hated what he'd just done.

His dire offense? Failure to use his blinker when changing lanes.

This particular day we were shuttling my mother-in-law to her doctor's appointment. When we arrived and took our place in the waiting room, my mind began to tally, one by one, other irksome things I didn't like about my man's behavior.

As each scenario popped into my mind, I grew more and more annoyed.

Across from me sat a chatty elderly woman. She spoke of some people all in a tizzy about the impending inclement weather, declaring they needed to remember one important fact: "Everybody's got somethin'."

I asked her just what she meant by that. "Well," she elaborated, "when we lived in Kansas, it was dust storms and tornadoes. Then the few years we lived in southern Florida, we had to prepare for hurricanes. And when we were stationed in California, oh, what a drought we had that one year. Like I say," she restated, "everybody's got somethin'."

My waiting-room friend's observation spiritually snapped me to attention that day. Why do I let certain aspects of my husband's personality bother me so easily? Surely I do things that drive him equally crazy!

"Everybody's got somethin'"—some behavior, quirk, practice, or habit that wreaks havoc on others, tempting them to become slightly irritated or even all-out furious.

Today's key verse states that "good sense makes one slow to anger," and that it is a person's "glory to overlook an offense" (Proverbs 19:11 ESV). In the original Hebrew language, the word *glory* conveys beauty, honor, splendor, and even adornment. Essentially, our patience in passing over an offense adorns us with true beauty and honors the other person.

Is there someone in your life who sometimes gets on your nerves or under your skin? How about trying a new approach—how about just keeping your cool? Don't say a word. Smile instead, and love despite a person's quirks.

Remember, everybody's got something.

Father, may I learn not to let the little quirks or even the bigger missteps of my loved ones provoke me to instant anger. Teach me to overlook an offense as I remember how much You've forgiven me. In Jesus' name, amen.

♾ Who sometimes bothers you with their behavior, and how can you overlook their offenses?

....

....

....

....

....

....

....

....

....

....

....

....

....

....

....

46

Being with God

Ruth

Whoever dwells in the shelter of the Most High
will rest in the shadow of the Almighty.

—PSALM 91:1

The mystery and beauty of God coming to us in Jesus is that He is God with us and for us. But He doesn't come close to us to keep us as we are. He comes to us, calls us, and graciously changes us from the inside out. The God who is with us and for us asks us a difficult question: *Are you with Me?*

I first noticed this theme in the Old Testament book of Joshua. It's a book that records Moses' successor, Joshua, leading the Israelites into the land of promise. Just as they were entering the land, they came to Jericho—a city of familiar reputation that would soon fall when they marched around it seven times! But before they entered the city and took their first steps toward witnessing God's promises fulfilled, God wanted them to think about where their loyalties were.

On his way to the city, Joshua encountered an unidentified man with his sword drawn—likely one of the angels of God's armies. Joshua wanted to know, "Are you for us or for our enemies?" (Joshua 5:13). The commander of the Lord's army gave a strange but important response. He simply said, "Neither" (v. 14).

You can imagine Joshua wondering, *Neither?* Not exactly the response he was expecting or hoping for. But with this response God wanted the Israelites to know this was His battle. God was going before them. He would be with them. The Lord wanted His people to know, as He still does today, that it is important we are with Him.

Do our attitudes, actions, and aspirations suggest we are really with God? Are our lives, with God's help, continuing to be refined? He is the center. We serve Him. Because He loves us, He wants to be the One leading us.

Whatever you are facing today, know that God is with you. His love is secure and His compassion unending. He will never leave you or forsake you. Today begin asking yourself these challenging questions: *Do I just want God to be with me and for me, doing what I ask? Or am I with God, willing to love and obey Him wherever He leads?*

Lord, Your ways and will are good, pleasing, and perfect. I know You are with me. You have saved me through the work of Your Son, Jesus. But You desire that I am with You, loving and obeying You. Help me keep Your will at the center of my life. In Jesus' name, amen.

- In what ways have you asked God to be with you instead of asking if you are with Him?
- Why is it so important to regularly ask yourself this question?

....

....

....

47

Build Bridges, Not Fences

Karen

We have this command from him: The one who loves
God must also love his brother and sister.

—1 JOHN 4:21 CSB

*L*ook, if this is going to be yet another call telling me I'm not obey-ing God, then I'm just going to politely hang up now, okay?"

The voice on the other end of the phone line was that of a new friend from church. She and her husband had just prayerfully opted to put their two formerly homeschooled kids in the neighborhood public elementary school. That morning—the first day of school—she had already fielded two calls from other women questioning her family's decision.

I had not called to give my friend a lecture. Not at all! Since my home was across the street from the kids' new school, I'd called to suggest that she put me down as an emergency contact in case one of them got sick or injured and she was unable to be reached.

"Also," I continued, "right now I can see both of your kids outside at recess playing on the monkey bars. They look like they are having a ball. I thought hearing that might set your mind at ease." My friend apolo-gized for her initial response, then she broke down and cried.

Schooling choices can divide people. So can politics. Or the choice of church denominations. Or lifestyle decisions such as the organic-only eaters from the fast-food brood. Different decisions can lead to many divisions.

Today's verse gives us a cautionary directive from God about how Christ-followers are to treat one another. "We have this command from him: The one who loves God must also love his brother and sister" (1 John 4:21 CSB).

What does it look like to love a fellow Christian who makes a choice that isn't a sin issue but is different from yours? Well, I know what it doesn't look like. It doesn't look like caustic and critical comments or behind-the-back gossip. It doesn't exclude someone once they've changed their work status from stay-at-home mom to full-time employee. And it certainly doesn't include making cloaked comments on social media designed to make someone else feel left out or somehow less than.

If we claim to love God, we must also love one another.

Life is a voyage packed with choices. Prayerfully supporting a friend's choice is a way to show unconditional love. While connections with other women in similar life situations can be crucial for idea gathering, perspective, and empathy, don't narrow your choice of friends down to only those who make all the same decisions you do.

Pick up the phone. Reach out. Build loving bridges, not barbed-wire fences. You'll obey God's command—and reflect His love—when you do.

Father, teach me to genuinely love and practically support others whose lives do not look exactly like mine. In Jesus' name, amen.

Is there anyone in your life who built a bridge toward you? How did it make you feel? Is there anyone you need to build a bridge toward?

48

It's Okay to Not Feel Okay

Ruth

"I will refresh the weary and satisfy the faint."

—JEREMIAH 31:25

*J*was tired of feeling like I had it all together. "I just need to be honest," I said to a friend. "I am wiped out. Exhausted. I need a break." My older and wiser friend gently responded, "It's okay to not feel okay. But let's not stay there."

I didn't want to stay there either. I had been running dangerously low on energy. Several project deadlines were looming. I hadn't cleared my email inbox in weeks. Our kids were running in every different direction with school and sports. You name it. I had a good excuse for feeling the way I did!

I was feeling the painful effects of self-neglect. It sounds silly now, but I almost felt guilty at the thought of taking time for myself. I was not okay, but was it really okay to hit pause? Pull away and do something for myself?

The answer is yes! It is not only okay; it's necessary to allow ourselves to be cared for. Renewed. Refreshed. God promises strength for the weary. Hope for the faint. It's okay not to feel okay. But God doesn't want us to stay there any more than we do.

The truth is, we are of little value to others when we are running on empty. When we are trapped in a cycle of sacrifice and self-neglect, it is nearly impossible to love God and love others well. We are at our best when we are living and loving out of a place of health—emotionally, physically, and spiritually.

If you are struggling with self-neglect, running on empty, and feeling like you're at the end of your rope, don't feel guilty about taking care of yourself. Get alone with God. Get away with some friends. Take time to do what energizes you most. Call a time-out! Ask for help. Whatever it takes, take some time just for you. When you do, you are in a far better place to love God and love others.

Father, You alone satisfy my soul. Your Word comforts me, and Your Spirit empowers me. In the places where I am weak and weary, give me renewed energy. Give me wisdom to know my limits. Teach me to rest in You and find time to allow You to love me, refill me, and teach me. In Jesus' name, amen.

❧ What are one or two things you can do to take time for yourself?
❧ Where do you need to ask for help in order to feel renewed or refreshed?

....

....

....

....

....

....

49

How to Manage Your Mountains

Karen

Yes, my soul, find rest in God; my hope comes from him. Truly he is my rock and my salvation; he is my fortress, I will not be shaken.

—PSALM 62:5–6

Some days it seems everywhere I look I see mountains—mountains of laundry to fold, papers to sort, emails to answer, and dirty dishes to clean. Tending to the mountains in my life often leaves me exhausted. It also triggers frustration because no sooner have I dealt with one of these mountains when another starts to pile up all over again, staring me in the face and leaving me defeated. Have you been there?

Our relationships also bring emotional mountains to scale as well. Constant interactions with people and the emotional stress they sometimes bring can make for a difficult climb. Perhaps a lesson on the sport of mountain climbing can give us insight into how to make our trek a little less daunting.

Mountain climbing is not for the faint of heart. Besides being physically strenuous, it causes changes in the climber's body as they ascend. The higher in elevation you go, the lower the oxygen concentration. If climbers aren't careful to take precautions, the change can cause serious medical conditions resulting in hospitalization and, in some cases, even death.

To prevent these conditions, an experienced mountain climber knows how important periods of rest are. And not just stopping at the current altitude to take a break. There is a strategy where climbers retreat to an elevation lower than the one to which they have climbed in order to give their lungs a rest—especially at night. This tactic is referred to as "climb high—sleep low." Mountaineers will trek as high as they safely can during the day but return to a lower elevation to sleep.

Similarly, the expedition known as life is not for the faint of heart. Although the highs and lows we traverse each day might not adversely affect our lungs, they can wreak havoc upon our hearts and drain us physically. Oh, how important it is to rest our bodies and nourish our souls!

Today's verse states it perfectly. When we carve out time to rest in God—taking a physical break and filling up our spirits—we gain hope and acquire strength to face the challenges of life.

Have you been trying to scale the mountain of life without stopping to refresh and refuel? Maybe it's time to adopt the "climb high—sleep low" strategy yourself.

As you trek onward and upward, God will be with you in the highs. He'll refresh you in the lows. Settle your soul and meet with Him today.

Father, please help me carve out time each week to get alone and
meet with You. May I find rest and rejuvenation so I can continue to
climb the mountains of life for Your glory. In Jesus' name, amen.

❧ What grade would you give yourself in the area of rest? What will
you do this week to carve out time to slow down and savor some
time alone with the Savior?

50

Costly Love

Ruth

This is how we know what love is: Jesus Christ laid down his life for
us. And we ought to lay down our lives for our brothers and sisters.

—1 JOHN 3:16

A friend of mine recently told me how she woke up in the middle of the night a bit disoriented but aware enough to know that God had a reason. As she began to pray, God brought to mind a friend she was having trouble loving and fully accepting.

Tell her she is My daughter too, she felt God saying. *If I love her, you can too.*

We all have those people, don't we? It's easy to love those we like. But real love, the kind of love Jesus demonstrated, is giving your life to someone for their betterment. It is good will. Action. Not for our sake, but for someone else's. It works, serves, endures, encourages, and forgives, all for the sake of seeing someone else grow and change for the better. It's not always what we get out of a relationship, but rather how we show and give the love of God to someone else.

Isn't this the way Jesus loves us? He loves us far more than we love Him back. He gives, and serves, and is patient with us. He works for our good, desiring to see lasting change that is marked by His Sprit at work in us. His love is costly. Sacrificial. Often one-sided. He is gentle with us, giving us room to grow up and be rooted in Him.

Loving those around us who are hard to love is impossible unless we anchor our lives in God's love. If we don't, we'll always be looking for a friend, coworker, or family member to love us back. But when we are receiving our love from God, His love frees us and empowers us to love others unconditionally.

Who in your life is hard to love? Where do you need to love others the way God has loved you? Someone in your life needs to know she is God's daughter too. Love her. Serve her. Accept her. Show her the kind of costly love Christ has shown you!

> Father, thank You for loving me unconditionally through Your Son. It is a costly and sacrificial love that led You to the cross. I was undeserving, unworthy, but You have loved me anyway. Help me love those around me with the same love You have shown me. In Jesus' name, amen.

∞ How can you begin to love even if it is hard?

∞ What is one way you can love someone for his or her sake and not your own?

....

....

....

....

....

51

A Dime in My Pocket

Karen

Have mercy on me, Lord, for I call to you all day long.

—PSALM 86:3

Do you remember pay phones? They used to hang on the walls at restaurants and airports, in shopping malls and at gas stations. When you needed to get a message to someone, you dug for the dime your mother (being the proper parent she was) always made sure resided in your jeans pocket. Then you reached for the receiver, slipped your other hand up to the slot, dropped the silver coin in, and dialed. Soon help, or a ride, was on the way.

I used my dimes sparingly when I was a kid in the 1980s, saving them for only completely necessary calls and occasional emergencies. In the course of a month, I resorted to using a reserved dime only a time or two. If a coin were to be used, I wanted to make sure it was really worth it. If not, it stayed conveniently tucked away in my front pocket, waiting for the day it would be called upon to rescue me.

Contrast this with communication on today's phones. We feel free to text, direct message, or contact someone through social media at the drop of a hat. It makes me think of our relationship with God. Hang with me, now.

I'm afraid that often I am much more like a teen in the '80s when it comes to calling upon the Lord. I reserve my spiritual dimes for the times when I really need Him, making sure it is worth the effort of prayer. When I fear I will be spiritually stranded without a ride, I call upon the Lord. Other times, sadly, I must admit my spiritual phone sometimes stays off.

Instead, I should feel free to message Him about any and everything and, as a result, stay constantly connected to Him throughout the course of my day. His line is never busy, and He longs to connect with me more than an occasional time or two a week. I too can call (pray), text (journal), save a message (memorize scripture), or return a message (praise Him) no matter the time or place! Oh, if only God's presence in our everyday lives became as precious and desired as our attachment to our phones!

How about it, fellow phoner? This week when we pick up our phones, let it trigger our memory of today's verse. Call upon the Lord. All day long. He will answer every time.

> Dear Lord, please forgive me for resorting to prayer only when I need You for something. I resolve now to keep connected with You all through my day. I'll call upon You in times of need as well as when I just want to thank You or spend time with You. You are my only lifeline. In Jesus' name, amen.

❧ When it comes to prayer, do you connect with God many times during the day, or are you more the dime-in-my-pocket sort of person? What is one action step you can take to spend more time with God?

....

....

....

52

Delivered from Temptation

Ruth

"Lead us not into temptation, but deliver us from the evil one."

—MATTHEW 6:13

Every day is a battle. It's not always a battle we see or understand. But because of our allegiance to Jesus, we are in a battle for our hearts and minds. Our Enemy would love nothing more than to disrupt, distract, and even destroy the good work God is doing in our lives.

We are tempted to despair.

Tempted to doubt.

We'd rather give up or give in.

We are tempted to coast.

Tempted to become weary.

We'd rather take it easy than be obedient.

Which is why Jesus, when He taught His disciples to pray, told them to pray for help in their times of weakness. In Matthew 6:13, Jesus said to pray, "Lead us not into temptation, but deliver us from the evil one." Is Jesus suggesting that God leads us into temptation? God certainly allows tests and trials into our lives for our good and for our growth. But God does not lead us toward sin or into sin (James 1:13).

Jesus was reminding us that every day really is a battle. Sin is up close and personal. It wages war against us and in us. We are to pray not to be enticed by sin when we encounter it. Jesus taught us to ask God for perspective. Wisdom. Protection. And most importantly, His power.

Where are you most tempted right now? What daily encounters have enticed you?

The good news is that we are not in this fight alone. The battle is not ours. It is God's. And He has given us everything we need in Christ to overcome the temptations we all face.

Remember, because we are in Christ, we don't fight for victory. We fight from a place of victory. Victory is already ours. Greater is He who is in us than He who is in the world (1 John 4:4).

So keep your eyes on Jesus. Root your life in His love. Be built up in the power that is yours in Christ. For He has promised to deliver you from every temptation.

Father, lead me not into temptation today. As I encounter sin, help me not be enticed by it. In Christ, You have already set me free from the power of sin. Your victory is mine. Fill me with Your strength and wisdom today as I seek to serve You in all I do. In Jesus' name, amen.

❧ Where are you most tempted right now?
❧ What is one way you can ask God to help you overcome sin?

....

....

....

....

53

R & R Required

Karen

> *The Lord is my shepherd, I lack nothing. He makes me lie down in*
> *green pastures, he leads me beside quiet waters, he refreshes my*
> *soul. He guides me along the right paths for his name's sake.*
>
> —Psalm 23:1–3

Are you an addict? I am. Sadly, my addiction is sometimes serious. And statistics indicate that many share my awful obsession. You see, I am addicted to busyness.

My habit began in high school. Yep, sign me up for sports, the school newspaper, foreign language club, youth group, volunteer work, and a part-time job to boot! By the time I graduated from high school, I was involved in more activities than a set of triplets should be. And unfortunately the busy buzz carried over into adulthood.

Current culture doesn't help. Society not only encourages a hectic lifestyle; it even applauds and rewards it! And what gal in her right mind doesn't want an "'atta girl" now and then?

To be effective women of God, however, we need to not only slow down, regularly scraping commitments off our too-full plates, but sometimes we need to cease the frenzy altogether.

I am just coming off a month-long internet break and social media fast. No status updates, posting cute pictures, or cruising the blogging superhighways for thirty-one days. It was both terribly hard and yet, in the end, wonderfully worth it.

For a few days during my break, I hunkered down at a local retreat center. Dorm-like with its cinder block rooms, it was very inexpensive and yet set in a lovely slice of nature: hills overlooking a grape arbor and a fragrant pear-and-apple orchard.

Even though it is nearly impossible to break away from life, I come here sometimes to get alone with God, to read, ponder, write, and reflect. I walk the white-pine and perennial-laced grounds in solitude. There are no blaring television sets, internet connections, or ringing phones—only unfamiliar but blessed quiet.

Christ beckoned us in Psalm 23:1–3 to lie down, to be led, to come have our souls refreshed. Don't miss that this passage states that the Lord "makes me lie down." We often don't slow ourselves down. Sometimes the Father needs to force us to do so for our own good. And most of all, it is necessary. When we retreat we can best hear from God, who often prefers not to scream over the noise of our busy lives, but instead gently whispers to us in the quiet solitude.

Yes, in the Christian life, retreat is required. Even Jesus Himself had regular times of rest and withdrawal. He leads by His example. Today why not consider a time, very soon, when you too will cease, retreat, and refuel? You won't regret it.

> Dear Lord, forgive me for ignoring Your command to come away
> with You for a while. Please arrange my circumstances so I might
> spend uninterrupted time with You. In Jesus' name, amen.

❧ When was the last time you completely unplugged from any screens and just got alone to be quiet and connect with God through prayer and reading your Bible? Carve out some time in the next few weeks to get alone, even if for a few hours. Put that time on your calendar right now, and be sure to follow through.

....

....

....

....

....

....

....

....

....

....

....

....

....

....

54

Do I Love God Enough?

Ruth

See what great love the Father has lavished on us, that we
should be called children of God! And that is what we are!

—1 JOHN 3:1

I have always been a rule follower. Things are pretty black and white
for me. For the most part, this is not always a bad thing. But sometimes I notice the faulty aspects of this part of my personality creeping
into my relationship with God. I can wrestle with whether or not I have
done enough for Him. Life can seem like a list of boxes I need to check in
order to love God enough.

There is no question that we are supposed to love God. We show our
love for God as we trust and obey Him. His commands are not burden-
some. We delight in doing what Jesus did because the truth lives in us.
But have you ever wrestled with whether or not you love God enough?

There have certainly been times in my own life when I didn't feel like
I was doing enough. Maybe my heart felt distant. The love I once had felt
like it had cooled off. It wasn't that I had walked away from my faith.
I was still reading my Bible, serving in my local church, and doing my
best, with God's help, to walk in obedience. But at times I've wondered if
it was all enough.

God had to remind me of a simple truth. What is far more important than whether I always feel like I have loved God enough is the fact that God loves me. The good news is good because through Christ God has done something for me that I could never do on my own. My acceptance was not based on what I did, but on what Jesus did for me. My salvation was by grace through faith.

And so I am learning to stress less about whether I have loved God enough. God's love for me is complete and final. Nothing can separate me from His love. Instead, I am choosing to rest in God's love for me. He loves me far more than I could ever love Him back. As much as I seek to love and obey God, it will always pale in comparison to how much He loves me!

> Father, thank You for loving me far more than I could ever love You back. You have saved me and forgiven me. You are changing me from the inside out. Teach me to rest in Your unconditional love. Help me love You back, not to earn Your love, but because I already have Your perfect love. In Jesus' name, amen.

- ❧ When and why have you wrestled with whether you love God enough?
- ❧ How does the cross change your motivation for obedience?

....

....

....

....

....

55

Does Practice Make Perfect?

Karen

Share with the Lord's people who are in need. Practice hospitality.

—ROMANS 12:13

You've no doubt heard the old adage, "Practice makes perfect." Teachers urge students to practice their penmanship. Bosses advise interns to practice their duties until they've sharpened their skills. And what former piano student can't still hear his or her teacher's voice echoing, "Practice, practice, practice"? But is it true that practice *always* makes perfect?

Tucked away in the New Testament book of Romans, God seems to have sent us a quick text message by way of a simple two-word sentence: "Practice hospitality" (Romans 12:13).

Notice that there is no mention of perfect. But the very word *hospitality* can evoke a feeling of panic and expectations of perfection. Pinterest images pop into our minds of magazine-like decor, gourmet-style fancy foods, spotless surroundings, and stunning homes. But do we, or our homes or food, have to be perfect in order to practice hospitality?

I find it interesting when studying the Bible not to look at just what a verse says but also at what it doesn't say. Today's key verse does not say many things. It does not say, "Now those of you who have roomy, gorgeous homes—complete with shiplap and subway tile—offer hospitality." There's no reference to the cleanliness of our homes, the decor on our walls, or our spatula-wielding expertise in the kitchen (or lack thereof). We are simply told to practice.

The verb *practice* is defined as "performing an activity repeatedly or regularly in order to improve one's proficiency." This definition doesn't state we will ever gain perfection, only that we will see progress.

When I became an adult living on my own, I swallowed hard, whispered a prayer, and began to open both my home and my heart. My practice has made progress. I have learned tips for decorating and methods for cleaning and gained an arsenal of easy, delicious dishes to offer guests.

But I have also served burned chicken, had company spy cobwebs on my light fixtures, and moved piles of unfolded laundry off the couch so guests could find a place to sit. Hospitality means being willing to welcome others into our lived-in homes and serve frozen pizzas and ice cream sandwiches with a smile.

Telling us to practice hospitality is one of God's ways of encouraging us to bless others, but often we end up blessed instead. Even with practice our houses, cuisine, and we ourselves may not be perfect, yet we'll be connecting hearts and touching lives as we seek to serve those God puts in our path. Put away the excuses and turn the coffee maker on. Company's coming!

> Dear Lord, forgive me for the times I've shied away from offering hospitality to others. Help me welcome and serve people as You have commanded me, knowing You are looking for progress, not perfection. In Jesus' name, amen.

❧ What is your go-to excuse for not having others over? How can you push past that and decide to offer imperfect hospitality to someone this week?

....

....

....

....

....

....

....

....

....

....

....

....

....

....

....

....

56

God Never Wastes Our Waiting

Ruth

We wait in hope for the LORD; he is our help and our shield.
In him our hearts rejoice, for we trust in his holy name.

—PSALM 33:20–21

"We wait in _____." I suppose there are a lot of ways to fill in the blank. We often wait in fear. We wait in anger. We wait in frustration or doubt. The bottom line is that most of us don't like to wait!

The Bible has a lot to say about waiting. Some of the great heroes of the faith were men and women who waited. Consider Abraham, Joseph, and David, just to name a few. And how about Sarah, Hannah, or Esther? They all waited. But how they waited made the difference.

What are you waiting on right now? Maybe you are waiting on a new job. A different job. You are waiting for a friend, coworker, or even spouse to change. You might be waiting on a pregnancy, a doctor's results, or a son or daughter to return to his or her faith. No matter the circumstances, we all face the same temptation in our waiting.

The temptation is often to get ahead of God. Rush His plan. Fast-forward His timing. We are tempted to be our own god, taking matters into our own hands.

But God never wastes our waiting. He does great work in the midst of our waiting. He teaches us humility, dependence on Him, and patience.

God refines us, purifying our selfish and sinful desires. Reminds us we serve Him and that His will really is good, pleasing, and perfect (Romans 12:2).

So if you are waiting, pay attention to how you wait. Remember that it is God you are waiting on. In Psalm 33:20, the psalmist told us that he waited "in hope for the LORD." Why? Because the Lord alone is "our help and our shield." His love is unfailing. His timing is perfect. And His waiting always comes with a promise—He will deliver. It might be different from what we expected or even wanted. But the Lord blesses those who wait on Him.

> Father, You alone are my help and my shield. I will wait on You. Give me strength to walk humbly and trust deeply. I know my waiting is never wasted by You. So continue the work You are doing in me, and draw me closer and deeper as I put my hope in You. In Jesus' name, amen.

∞ When have you gotten ahead of God's timing or plan?

∞ How have you seen God bless your waiting?

....

....

....

....

....

....

57

Just Nine Doors Down

Karen

"Love your neighbor as yourself."

—MARK 12:31

*I*n the two years since we'd moved into our new neighborhood, I'd seen her during my walks. Sometimes she was rolling her trash can out to the curb or watering her flowers. I'd smile and say hi for a brief second. After all, the neighborhood is big; my life is busy. So I'd pop my earbuds back in and keep walking to my house, just nine doors down.

A while back, there were flashing lights and sirens in my neighborhood. *A fire, maybe?* I thought. Although the rescue vehicles were parked in front of my nine-doors-down neighbor's house, no fire appeared to blaze. *Must have been a false alarm*, I reasoned to myself.

Two days later I heard the awful news. No fire. No smoke. Just a terribly saddened soul.

You see, just nine doors down, something happened in the mind of my nameless, flower-watering fellow human being. Something told her this life wasn't worth living anymore. And she agreed.

Now her heart no longer beats. I can still walk by her house, lost deeply in the Jesus-music blaring from my phone. Rushing to the next thing on my to-do list for the day.

Nine doors down there will be no more waves, smiles, or thoughts of, *I should stop and find out her name.* If I'd reached out and befriended her, would she have seen Jesus through our friendship? Would a glimpse of the perfect God in the life of an imperfect me have beckoned her to have a relationship with Him too? Would she have found God's purpose and peace instead of finding a way to end her emotional pain? Only God knows.

I am a woman who wants to love God, but so often I am too busy to really love the people He puts plainly in my path. God calls us to love our neighbor. But to do that, we first need to notice them and get to know them. Even though our schedules are full, we can pause, permitting God to tap us on the heart, gently interrupt us, and rearrange our day. When God knocks on our hearts, we can knock on their doors. Then once we've reached out, we leave the outcome to Him.

May we all respond to those taps on our hearts today and not ignore them. God just may use us as He saves a life. It might not even be much of a walk . . . even just nine doors down.

> Dear Lord, I want to be aware of the times You tap my heart,
> asking me to reach out to someone. May I pay attention and
> respond so he or she might know You. In Jesus' name, amen.

❧ Is there someone in your path whom you feel God may be calling you to reach out to but you've been too busy to respond to His nudge? Who is it, and how will you show kindness to him or her this week?

....

....

....

58

In Over Your Head

Ruth

*The LORD said to Gideon, "You have too many men. I
cannot deliver Midian into their hands, or Israel would
boast against me, 'My own strength has saved me.'"*

—JUDGES 7:2

We've all been there. A new job, different season, or set of circumstances in which we felt in over our head. Gideon, one of Israel's judges in the Old Testament, was no exception. He was tasked with leading the Israelites against one of their enemies, the Midianites.

It seemed Israel had more than enough fighting men, with a rather large and robust army. So their task was manageable. Doable. Not too terribly scary. Until the Lord told Gideon to send tens of thousands of fighting men home. Why?

In Judges 7:2, the Lord told Gideon he had "too many men." If they went to war and won, they would think it was in their own strength. Their own power and resourcefulness would get the glory. They'd say, "My own strength has saved me." So God whittled down their army to just a few hundred men. Victory would be theirs, but ultimately the victory would be God's!

It seems that often times, when we feel in over our heads, we are exactly where God wants us. When we feel overwhelmed by a new job, maybe a ministry position at church, or a new opportunity, the feeling of being in over our heads might be exactly where God wants us because it is no longer about us.

When we feel in over our heads, we have no choice but to trust God. To seek His wisdom. To cling to His promises of faithfulness and power. In other words, when we feel unprepared, overwhelmed, or underqualified, we are in a great position for God to get the glory He deserves.

So don't be afraid to prayerfully try something new. Don't be discouraged or worried about being in too deep or in over your head. You just might be exactly where you are supposed to be. Let God be the One to come through and the One to get the praise!

Lord, I need Your strength. You alone are the One who gives me power, wisdom, and victory. Would You go before me, lead me, and give me all I need to accomplish what You have called me to? I trust You. I am looking to You. Help me live for Your glory and not my own. In Jesus' name, amen.

Where do you feel in over your head?

How has fear of failure kept you from obeying God?

59

Shaping Your Home

Karen

My salvation and glory depend on God, my
strong rock. My refuge is in God.

—PSALM 62:7 CSB

They piled high on the living room coffee table: colorfully wrapped boxes with curly, coordinating bows and snappy gift bags with crisp tissue paper peeking out of their tops in anticipation. They accented the festivities as nearly three dozen friends eagerly gathered for an open house for my friend Thida.

A Cambodian native, Thida met my friend Keith when he was studying abroad in her country. Now they were married and living in the United States, and our circle of friends threw her an old-fashioned housewarming party.

What domestic treasures she opened that night! Fluffy new towels, spice-scented candles, picture frames, and pots. Ever a soft-spoken and grateful person, she was visually humbled and verbally thankful with each package she unwrapped. Every so often she would look at the crowd and utter the same phrase: "Oh . . . I want to thank you so much for helping me to shape our home."

We knew what Thida meant. She meant to furnish her home, to decorate and outfit it with needed and useful items. But somehow when trying to get her sentiments across by speaking in English (her second language), the phrase she continually chose was "shape our home."

As I heard sweet Thida utter these words many times that night, it struck a chord within me. In essence, this group of siblings, aunts, cousins, and grandparents by marriage, along with an abundance of new friends, were helping to do exactly that!

Thida began a relationship with Jesus because of the example of an aunt who taught her what it means to follow Him. Rather than choosing the false god that many of her ancestors followed, she chose the true God of the Bible. Now she and her husband desire to walk with God, and we, as her circle of support in her new country of residence, will try our best to encourage her in her endeavors. Yes, you could say in essence that we all have made a covenant to help Thida do exactly what she said—shape her home.

Do you know another woman who has made a decision for Christ? One who left her former ways to walk in the ways of the Lord? If so, there are eyes upon you, watching, soaking in, and learning. What will she see? Will you help her shape her heart's home with God's truths while building on the foundations of Christ?

Home shaping is significant business. May we all be mirrors that reflect Christ to those who are watching, soaking in, learning, and yes, perhaps even shaping.

Dear Lord, may I be ever mindful there are others looking to me for an example of how to shape our lives according to Your ways. In Jesus' name, amen.

❧ Think of someone you know who has recently begun to be interested in learning about what it means to walk with Jesus.

What can you do to help her shape her faith and respond to the truth of the gospel?

....

....

....

....

....

....

....

....

....

....

....

....

....

....

....

....

60

Reading It Again

Ruth

Trouble and distress have come upon me, but
your commands give me delight.

—PSALM 119:143

A few years ago during a weekend retreat, a youth leader wrote our daughter a special note. Filled with words of encouragement and truth, it was a breath of fresh air for our daughter. She read it and reread it countless times, hanging on every word.

On our drive home from the weekend retreat, I looked in the rearview mirror to find my daughter reading the note . . . again! "You're reading it again?" I asked her. "Yes, Mom," she responded. "I need to because I don't remember everything she said."

As we continued our drive home that Sunday night, it hit me that God's Word is like that. We too need to be reminded of what it says. We read it and read it again. We keep coming back to it over and over because we need the reminder of who God is and who we are.

God is good and faithful. He really has spoken. He loves us. He is with us. He has given His Word as a source of great strength, wisdom, and hope. I need it today just as much as I did when I first received it.

When life gets hard or stressful, it's so tempting to turn elsewhere. To forget God's truth. But every other source leaves us empty, never satisfying our souls. Think for a moment of what the Bible says about itself:

- ❧ The Bible is pure (Psalm 19:8 ESV).
- ❧ It is a guide for life (Psalm 119:105).
- ❧ God's Word feeds and nourishes our souls (Jeremiah 15:16).
- ❧ It changes us (Hebrews 4:12).
- ❧ The Bible is true (John 17:17 and 2 Timothy 3:16).
- ❧ It purifies us from sin (Ephesians 5:26).

The Bible is worth reading again and again. God wants to remind you of His love. To encourage you with His promises. To guide you with His truth. It's easy to forget, so we need to keep coming back to the God who reminds us in the most perfect way.

> Father, I praise You because You have spoken. You have given me Your Word. Your truth and promises are a delight to me. They bring me joy and hope. Help me reflect deeply on who You are. Teach me to treasure all You have done for me in Christ. I need the reminder as much today as when I first began to walk with You. In Jesus' name, amen.

- ❧ What keeps you from reading God's Word more often?
- ❧ What is one way you can begin making God's Word more of a priority in your life?

....

....

....

61

Answer the Call

Karen

Answer me when I call to you, my righteous God. Give me relief
from my distress; have mercy on me and hear my prayer.

—PSALM 4:1

Ughhh!" I sighed as my phone buzzed that morning—again. I'd already responded to several texts and phone calls, and it wasn't even noon yet! My mind and my heart began to race. *When am I ever going to get to the bottom of my never-ending to-do list?*

I glanced at my phone to see who it was this time. The number on my screen was a familiar one—that of my father. He is a retiree who has lots of time on his hands. I reasoned that, since his schedule isn't nearly as full as mine, I could call him back later at a time more convenient for me. So I ignored his call and turned my attention back to my to-do list.

On it were many tasks, many of them mundane. But there were also some kingdom-building ministry activities: finish my Bible study lesson and pray for a friend's operation taking place later that day. Yes, my day was full—full of people and purpose. Why, then, did I feel so empty?

My thoughts returned to the call from my father. How many times had I ignored his calls, reasoning that since his life as a retiree wasn't packed with activity, I could easily chat with him later? But that often meant he took a place on the back burner of my life. He was waiting; I was ignoring.

It isn't just earthly fathers who sometimes get ignored. How many times have we put our heavenly Father on the back burner because of our screaming schedules and earthly relationship demands?

Today's verse paints a picture of our loving God who is never too busy to answer us when we call. And He not only hears and answers. He is calling. We ignore. The problem in our connection lies with us.

God is waiting and longing to have a deep, intimate relationship connection with us—one that requires we make one simple switch: we put Him at the top of our to-do and our must-call lists.

He is willing to answer, if only we will call.

Dear Lord, forgive me for ignoring Your calls to come and connect with You, free from any distractions. I'm ready now. Speak. I'm listening. In Jesus' name, amen.

❧ Do you make it a priority to answer when you sense God calling you to put down your task list and connect with Him? How can you improve in this area?

....

....

....

....

....

....

62

When God Doesn't Do What You Want

Ruth

James and John, the sons of Zebedee, came to him. "Teacher,"
they said, "we want you to do for us whatever we ask."

—MARK 10:35

The disciples were on their way to Jerusalem. Struggling to understand all Jesus was telling them about what awaited Him, James and John made one of the Bible's boldest statements to Jesus. It is also one of the worst!

Jesus had just told them that He must go to Jerusalem to be handed over and condemned to death. This was not the first time they had heard Jesus talk like this. The good news, He told them, was that He would rise again. Like many of the Jews at the time, James and John thought they were coming into their glory. God was going to throw off their enemies. Restore Israel. Bring peace. And they were going to be, or at least wanted to be, right at the center of it all.

Barely missing a beat, James and John's first response to what Jesus had just told them was, "We want you to do for us whatever we ask" (Mark 10:35). A pretty bold request! Of course, they wanted Jesus to exalt them to a position of power or status. They wanted to rule with Jesus. And yet Jesus reminded them that they must first suffer for Him.

God was not going to do what they wanted.

It's easy to poke holes in James and John's request and miss the more discreet ways we try to sell our own agendas to God. We too come to Jesus with our big plans, expectations, and self-centered dreams. When God doesn't do what we want, we are tempted to get angry, lose faith, or take matters into our own hands.

The Bible says, "Many are the plans in a person's heart, but it is the Lord's purpose that prevails" (Proverbs 19:21). Today, posture your heart to do what God wants. Walk humbly. Remember that He is the One leading you.

When God doesn't do what we want, He is doing something better.

Lord, You are the King of creation. Reign in my life. Humble me. Posture my heart to do what You want. Forgive me for the times I make conditions or demands. You are the center, and I am not. I want to follow You, knowing that where and how You lead me is better and wiser. In Jesus' name, amen.

- How have you made the same request as James and John?
- What "agenda" do you need to turn from in order to posture your heart to do God's will?

....

....

....

....

....

....

63

Who Will You Invite?

Karen

A father to the fatherless, a defender of widows, is God in his holy dwelling. God sets the lonely in families.

—PSALM 68:5–6

*I*t's the most wonderful time of the year!" The store's loudspeaker blared the joyful lyrics of the familiar song that snowy Christmas Eve afternoon.

Everywhere I glanced, people were searching for last-minute gift purchases, holiday baking ingredients, or that one final string of twinkle lights that would make their Christmas downright Norman Rockwell perfect. But as I stood in line to pay for the ingredients for my assigned cheesy-potato casserole for our family gathering, a lump formed in my throat.

How can everyone be so happy? Why is the world going on as if nothing happened? My friend Julie died last night, leaving behind a husband and eight children who need her. Doesn't anyone care?

I wanted to scream. And I wanted the holidays to be canceled that year. There was no cheer in me, and I thought the rest of the world should follow suit and just "humbug" the whole celebration.

Ever since that year our family has become more aware of the fact that, for many people, holidays *aren't* the most wonderful times of the year. In fact, they can be downright painful. While scores of us delight in the season, drinking in the sights, sounds, and smells, others are numb from pain and despise these months.

A neighbor of mine had a good perspective on helping those who hurt. She once told me, "Holidays are an excuse for making someone's life better." She was right! People are waiting to be encouraged and included—even during the time of Fourth of July picnics or potentially lonely Valentine's Day evenings. If only we would cease our own self-focused hustle and bustle long enough to see!

When we are intent on being Jesus' hands and feet to others, God will allow us to brighten the lives of many. We get to show His love and character talked about in Psalm 68:5–6—a God who is concerned about the loneliness of others and takes action to alleviate it. We can welcome others into our lives, allowing them to share a meal, a cup of coffee, or just share some time talking.

Let's use holidays and special occasions—even minor ones—as an excuse to make other people's days brighter, letting them know they are noticed and cared for.

Dear Lord, show me who needs to be reached out to this Thanksgiving and Christmas season. Help me make someone's life richer, fuller, and far less lonely. I want to be Your hands and feet. In Jesus' name, amen.

❧ Look at your calendar. Is there a holiday or special occasion coming up when you could invite over someone who might normally be alone that day? What can you do to encourage that person and brighten his or her day?

64

Being Refined

Ruth

It was good for me to be afflicted so that I might learn your decrees.

—PSALM 119:71

The real test of the depth of our faith is when we suffer. It's easy to love and serve God when things are going well. But come a little rain, some turbulence, or a few hills, and many of us begin to discover what we really believe, or don't believe, about God.

Difficult and sometimes dark times are not to be celebrated. Nobody, at least in their right mind, should rejoice *for* the opportunity to suffer! But we can and should rejoice *in* our suffering (James 1:2–3). Why? Because God uses tough seasons and circumstances to do some of His greatest work in us.

Trials or suffering don't guarantee that we will grow. Growing through our suffering requires some choices. We have to decide: *What will I do with this season? How will I respond to these circumstances? Does God just want me to get through it or grow through it?*

The decision is ours to make. We can either resist what God is really doing in our suffering or embrace it. Learn from it. Surrender. Trust God no matter what. Stay faithful.

There is no greater example in the Bible or in history of how to suffer the right way than the example of Jesus. Of course, He didn't need to overcome a sin nature. He was the perfect and sinless Son of God. But He did show us how to suffer the right way, with God's help.

The writer of Hebrews said, "Son though he was, he learned obedience from what he suffered" (5:8). Jesus didn't sin when He suffered. He entrusted Himself to the Father's perfect love and will. He remained obedient. He did not swerve to the left or the right. He was faithful, even to the point of death.

What God is really doing in our suffering is refining us. Making us new. He is teaching us to anchor our lives to what matters most, in what truly lasts.

Will you let Him? Will you surrender to the soul-shaping, eternity-lasting work of God's hand even when it is hard?

> Father, I know You love me. But Your love is not content to keep me where I am. Even in trials You are shaping me for my good and Your glory. Help me surrender. Teach me to walk faithfully and humbly with You. Don't just change me; change all of me. In Jesus' name, amen.

- Where are you most tempted to doubt God in your suffering?
- How can you practically surrender or cooperate with what God is really doing?

....

....

....

....

65

That Time I Just Couldn't Shut Up

Karen

*Do you see someone who speaks in haste? There
is more hope for a fool than for them.*
—PROVERBS 29:20

*H*as your mouth ever gotten you in trouble—yes, even made you sin—all because you talked too much? It's certainly happened to me!

Years ago while visiting with a friend during a high school basketball game, we discussed a budding new relationship between our seventeen-year-olds—her son and my daughter. It was nothing official, but we knew they liked each other.

I rattled on about how my husband and I worked hard to teach our kids to choose whom to date, or even marry, based on more than just their looks. We'd often joke that looks shouldn't matter since we're all headed toward ugly anyway.

In trying to express how happy we were that our daughter listened to us and chose someone who was not *only* good-looking but *also* displayed godly traits and had a wonderful personality, somehow my friend thought I was saying we were glad our daughter chose based on character because—boy, was her son homely!

It wasn't until a few days later that I realized I had conveyed the wrong sentiment. I received a message from my friend stating how hurt she was by my backhanded compliment about her son's character, implying he was unattractive.

I was devastated. I felt misunderstood. And I had a fractured friendship with someone I'd really hoped to get to know better. All because of my words.

Immediately I called to apologize and shared what I meant to say before my rambling thoughts came out as misspoken words—that then led to misunderstanding, conflict, and offense. Thankfully she accepted my apology, and years later, we are still friends!

If we want to avoid offending others—or committing any number of verbal sins—we need to learn to control our words. When we sense a gentle nudge from the Holy Spirit that signals a downward spiral, we can simply say, "I'm sorry. I'm talking too much."

In order not to speak in haste, as cautioned against in today's verse, we need to pause. To ponder. To shoot up a quick prayer asking God to help us choose which words, if any, to speak. Giving thoughts time to settle and soak in Scripture is a wonderful habit that will keep us from answering too soon and looking foolish.

So pause. Think before you answer, and don't speak your words in haste and risk fracturing a relationship.

Father, I want to reflect Your love and grace each time I open my mouth to speak. Help me slow my tongue before I say something hurtful that can have lasting consequences. And when I fall short, help me be quick to seek forgiveness and reconciliation. In Jesus' name, amen.

How would you rate yourself on a scale from one to ten when it comes to speaking in haste? If one means you always carefully weigh your words and ten means you speak quickly before thinking, what number would you choose? Now, what can you tell yourself as you are conversing with others that will help you lower that number?

....

....

....

....

....

....

....

....

....

....

....

....

....

....

66

Would You Follow You?

Ruth

Follow my example, as I follow the example of Christ.

—1 CORINTHIANS 11:1

Friendships are not optional in the Christian life. They are necessary for sustaining us through all that life throws at us. We see the perfect picture of community in God as Father, Son, and Spirit. Joined together in oneness, love, and intimacy, our need for community mirrors the very nature of who God was, is, and always will be. We were created for deep and meaningful community.

But as much as friendships can be a gift, they can also be dangerous. The very relationships God invites us into as places of refuge, acceptance, support, and encouragement can turn into ripe environments for dragging us down.

Our closest friendships are usually with the people we feel most comfortable around. We let our guard down. Feel safe to be who we really are. While these are good qualities in a friendship, we can also lose sight of the truth that we are called to raise up those we are in relationships with. It can be easy to let friendships become a swamp of gossip, selfishness, and an inward focus if we aren't careful.

So don't lose sight of the real goal of friendship—becoming more like Christ. Community itself is not the end goal. It is a means to growth and maturity. God wants to use you as the kind of friend others want to be like. A friend others want to follow. His heart for you in friendship is to be loved and encouraged for sure, but He also wants you to elevate those around you.

Jesus didn't just create a community. He was on mission. He invited others to join Him on a journey of living for God's purpose and glory in the world. As the apostle Paul did, we can humbly invite others to follow our example as we follow the example of Christ (1 Corinthians 11:1).

Are you making those around you better, more like Christ? Or have you become too comfortable in your friendships, letting others drag you down? Here is a question to wrestle with, pray about, and strive to answer with the help of God's Spirit at work in you. If you weren't you, would you follow you?

> Lord, I love You and praise You for Your grace. Thank You for saving
> me and calling me into friendship with You. Give me wisdom
> to grow into being the kind of friend worth following. Help me
> see my friendships differently and know the significance of my
> role. I want to follow the example of Jesus as I strive to be an
> example to those who are following me. In Jesus' name, amen.

- ❧ Where have you noticed the tendency to become too comfortable in friendships?
- ❧ What needs to change most right now in order for you to become a friend worth following?

....

....

67

Stay Home and Change the World

Karen

He said to them, "Go into all the world and
preach the gospel to all creation."
—MARK 16:15

When I was sixteen years old, I wanted to change the world. I'd just begun my relationship with God after being introduced to Him at a youth retreat. Soon afterward, I started attending a missions-minded church. They told stories of people in far-off lands who needed to hear about Jesus.

My plan was to someday go far away and help. Maybe I'd take clean water or medicine or teach others a new skill. But more than anything, I wanted to tell people about the gospel of Jesus, introducing them to the God I loved and the Bible I couldn't put down. That was my plan . . . or so I thought.

Instead, today I work from home with a limited budget, a used computer, and yet an unchanged desire. I still want to change lives with the love of Christ. Thankfully, He's shown me I don't need to leave home to do that.

And you don't either. We can change the world from our very own homes, in our very own neighborhoods. All we need is a desire to tell the good news and some means of connecting with others online. It's an easy way to be part of the charge in Mark 16:15 to "go into all the world and preach the gospel to all creation." We women can band together to tell the world about Jesus by holding a local Bible study or women's group or even by linking up with others online to share biblical content on a website or social media site.

The internet is a powerful entity. It can be used for evil, or it can be used to do great good. God is doing exciting things all over the world. If you can't travel somewhere physically to help, you can still give of your time by praying for ministries and organizations that are having an impact on the world for good and for God. Or you can give financially, even if it just means selling some gently used clothing and accessories and then donating the proceeds to one such charity.

We might not be building wells to provide clean water, but we can give women stuck in sadness or sin hope of a life in Christ by partnering with an organization that spreads the gospel. We might not be dispensing medicine ourselves, but we can give financially and prayerfully to organizations that do or to those who point women to the Healer who can make their spirits whole.

Do you want to change the world by offering hope, help, and even life from your home? When we give our collective "littles"—from our own little homes—God transforms them into a big movement that will alter lives both now and for eternity.

Dear Lord, thank You for the countless blessings You give me every day.
Food. Shelter. Family. Friends. Please take my little, transform it with Your
touch, and use it to bring more people into Your kingdom as they experience
and respond to the good news of Christ. In Jesus' name, amen.

❧ Take some time today to research some organizations and ministries that are making a lasting impact for God's kingdom by spreading the gospel and meeting the physical needs of others. Look for ways to partner with them both financially and spiritually to help bring change in the world today.

....

....

....

....

....

....

....

....

....

....

....

....

....

....

68

A Different Kind of Peace

"Peace I leave with you; my peace I give you. I do not give to you as the world gives. Do not let your hearts be troubled and do not be afraid."

—JOHN 14:27

I tiptoed out of our room, careful not to wake our youngest daughter who had joined us in the middle of the night. She has a keen sense for knowing when I get up. I'm not a morning person, but sometimes getting up early is about the only shot I have at some peace and quiet.

I made my coffee, planted myself in my favorite spot on the couch, grabbed my Bible and journal, and began to read. Things were quiet. Really quiet. And peaceful. But it lasted only about fifteen minutes! As soon as my peace had come, it quickly disappeared. Our kids were waking up. The dog needed go out. A new day was officially in front of me. This kind of peace is always fleeting, and it's far from the kind of peace Jesus offers us.

Jesus gives us a different kind of peace. He tells us in John 14:27 that the peace He gives us is not like the world's peace. The kind of peace the world offers comes and goes. That kind of peace or assurance is temporary, often tethered loosely to things like money, status, relationships, or health. Or a quiet cup of coffee before anyone else is awake!

No, the peace Jesus gives us is peace with God. It's a deep and abiding sense that everything is okay, and is going to be okay, because of who we belong to.

I am God's daughter. Saved and forgiven. I belong to His kingdom. And no matter what happens in life, God is with me.

"Do not let your hearts be troubled and do not be afraid," Jesus said in John 14:27. Jesus offers us a different kind of peace—a peace that goes beyond our understanding. A peace that guards our hearts and minds from fear or worry. A peace He gives when we ask for it.

Will you rest in it today?

> Father, thank You for the gift of Your Son, Jesus. Even though I was once Your enemy, You have made peace with me through the cross. The peace You give is assurance and hope. You have loved me and saved me. Nothing in life or death can separate me from You. Guard my heart and mind from fear and worry. Give me Your peace today. In Jesus' name, amen.

❧ Where do you most often look to find peace?

❧ How is the peace that Jesus gives so different from the world's?

....

....

....

....

....

....

....

69

Lumped Together

Karen

Let everyone see that you are considerate in all you
do. Remember, the Lord is coming soon.

—PHILIPPIANS 4:5 NLT

I cringe at generalizations and stereotypes. Lumping an entire group of people into a confining box. Like "The _____ (nationality or race) are so _____ (bad character trait)" or "Those _____ (age group, gender, or economic level) all are so _____ (strange habit or behavior)." However, every once in a while, being lumped together can be quite the compliment.

Recently as I waited in line at a coffeehouse, a frail, elderly woman stood in front of me ordering a meal. She seemed distressed as she fumbled for her change, paid the worker, and then gathered up her bag of food and her drink. As she headed for the door, her large purse began swinging off of her shoulder, nearly knocking her and all of her lunch to the floor.

"Oh . . . how am I going to do this? Oh my . . . oh dear . . . I can't . . . ," she mumbled to herself, trying to shift her weight and her cargo while pushing open the door at the same time.

Though I'd just finally reached the front of the line, God used today's verse to tap me on the heart and shift my momentary schedule. I quickly hopped out of line.

"Here, let me get that for you," I said as I held the door open and steadied her drink. "Would you like me to carry your food to your car?" She stopped in her tracks, her bright blue eyes looking up at me with gratefulness. "Oh dear . . . you must have a grandmother still living that you're so kind to an old woman."

"No, ma'am, I don't," I answered. "I just love Jesus, and He wants me to help you."

Her face softened. She shook her head and decidedly declared, "Of course! You people have always been so helpful to me. I don't know what I'd do without you."

You people. I'm pretty sure she meant, "You Christians." It made me wonder how other Christians had helped her. Did they take her a meal? Rake her yard in the fall or shovel her driveway in the winter? Had they driven her to a doctor's appointment? It reminded me of the age-old truth: more is caught than taught. And it demonstrated to me that people are watching—and lumping.

What do others see in us? Do they see us being considerate in all we do? If people are watching and all they see are uncaring, condemning, or even combative Christians, why would they ever want to become one?

Let's make it our prayer today that we, as Christ-followers, will be lumped in the "you people" group my new coffeehouse friend saw. Considerate Christians who make God and His body of believers look good.

People are watching. And lumping. What will they see in you?

Dear Lord, forgive me for the times when I choose condemnation over love or rudeness over kindness or decide to do nothing rather than do the right thing. Please prompt my heart and interrupt my momentary schedule so my actions accurately reflect who You are. In Jesus' name, amen.

❧ As you go about your day today, be on the lookout for someone you can bless with a thoughtful gesture, kind word, or good deed. When they thank you, give all the credit to the Lord. Write about your experience below.

....

....

....

....

....

....

....

....

....

....

....

....

....

70

When You Feel Unseen

*The eyes of the L*ORD *are on those who fear him, on those whose*
hope is in his unfailing love, to deliver them from death.

—PSALM 33:18–19

J was in a hurry to finish a few things on my computer before we left. The kids were picking up the family room. My husband was looking for the keys to the car.

"I'm almost ready," I announced to everyone. "Just give me five more minutes!" And then I heard our youngest daughter's enthusiastic voice.

"Mom, Mom, look at this!" I heard her, but I was on a mission. Her voice grew a little bit louder. *"Mom,* watch this!" I looked up, just in time to miss it. "Did you see it?" she asked. With a yo-yo dangling from her hand, she had just successfully completed a new trick she had just learned. And I missed it! She did it again. This time I was sure to keep my eyes on her.

My kids are a constant reminder of just how much we desire to be seen. To be known. To have someone delight in what we do or who we are. And their desire is really the same as ours. A longing to know we serve a God who is not easily distracted or too busy to notice us, care for us, or just take pleasure in us.

The psalmist said the "eyes of the LORD are on those who fear him, on those whose hope is in his unfailing love" (Psalm 33:18). Do you believe that? Are you convinced that God is not too busy for you? That His eyes are really on you?

In Christ, He looks on us with love, approval, and joy. He sees us in those times and seasons when it is tempting to think no one else does. As we look to God, He is looking upon us.

Maybe you are in a season when you feel like no one notices what you're doing. Perhaps you are waiting on God to show up and answer your prayers. Be encouraged that God has not left you. He is not distracted or too busy for you. And He certainly has not forgotten you. You are not alone, for God sees you through the lens of His love.

Father, thank You that You really do see me. You notice me. Delight in me. You have not forgotten me, and You are never too busy for me. Remind me that I am not alone. Encourage me with the truth that no matter what others see, You see me completely. You look on me with love and acceptance. In Jesus' name, amen.

∞ In what ways do you seek out the "eyes" of others?
∞ Where do you need the reminder that the "eyes of the LORD" are on you?

....
....
....
....
....

71

Friendly, Not Feisty

Karen

She opens her mouth with wisdom, and the teaching of kindness is on
her tongue. She looks well to the ways of her household and does not
eat the bread of idleness. Her children rise up and call her blessed.

—PROVERBS 31:26–28 ESV

On a sunny spring day, I sat in my backyard with a friend and all of our kids. The children were happily creating masterpieces in coloring books while sipping lemonade.

When it came time to clean up and go inside, I spied a frightful sight. One of my friend's daughters had grabbed permanent markers from my house to color with instead of the crayons. And colored with them she did—all over our brand-new picnic table! She'd even written her name in her very best seven-year-old penmanship.

I was angry that our newly purchased table was now laden with red and purple permanent graffiti. I wanted to raise my voice and shout and scream my displeasure. But I didn't. Instead, I leaned over and gently spoke to my friend's child.

"Oh, Kelly. Miss Karen wants you to use crayons when you color, not markers. Would you please go put them back in the house? Thank you, honey."

My eldest child's jaw dropped when she saw how I reacted to the situation with kindness and a calm voice. Loud enough for everyone to hear, she said, "Man! It's a good thing it was you, Kelly, and not one of us. Mom would've hollered at us something awful if we'd done that!"

Ouch.

My daughter simply vocalized a truth she noticed in my life: I tend to lose my cool with those who live within the same four walls as I do, but somehow I manage to keep calm when I interact with others.

Today's verse, describing the actions of the woman from Proverbs 31:26 (ESV), states, "She opens her mouth with wisdom, and the teaching of kindness is on her tongue." Can that be said of us? Or would a reality TV reporter capture the way we talk to our families or roommates and announce, "She snaps with caustic words, and 'Why can't you *this?*' and 'You should have *that!*' rolls angrily off her tongue." Is that how the woman written about in this verse spoke?

No. She spoke with kindness—the tone of voice you'd use with a stranger. She was friendly, not feisty.

I faced the music that day and owned up to the truth my child pointed out. Perhaps we would all do better to learn to pause before we pounce when interacting with our loved ones, treating them with the respect we tend to give others. Let's all purpose to be friendly—and not feisty—with those we live with today.

Dear Lord, I want to love people well, but as I seek to do so, help me pause before I react, to ensure my words and actions are pleasing to You. In Jesus' name, amen.

&. Is there someone in your life with whom you recently were more feisty than friendly? Write out a sentence prayer here asking God to forgive you for your unkind behavior. Then—deep breath—reach out to that person to admit your fault and ask for forgiveness.

....

....

....

....

....

....

....

....

....

....

....

....

....

....

....

....

....

....

72

Not Ruled by Emotions

You have been set free from sin and have become slaves to righteousness.

—ROMANS 6:18

*E*motions can get a bad rap. And although I have found myself time and again having to keep my emotions in check when they would love to rule over me, the truth is that emotions are not the enemy. God wired us to think, feel, and act. But what we *do* with those emotions determines their significance.

The book of Psalms is a great example of how God is big enough to handle our honest, and often raw, emotions. Burying our emotions can be dangerous to our souls. But becoming a slave to how we feel is even more dangerous.

We can let unresolved anger or bitterness slowly eat away at our joy and peace. We can let fear steal our contentment. We can let pity parties keep us from loving others the way Christ has loved us. Or unresolved hurts from the past can follow us into the future—leading us to repeat the same sins of those who came before us.

The good news is this: we have been set free from sin—including the sin of letting our emotions rule us.

In the Bible, sin is often described as separation. Our sin can separate us from loving God and loving others. But sin is also described as slavery. Any sin or unchecked emotion can control us, promising things it can never deliver.

The apostle Paul reminded us of the good news in Romans 6:18. Even though the presence of sin is real, Jesus has broken the power of sin. We sin not because we have to, but because we choose to. We are set free to love and serve God, a Ruler who brings about love and joy and peace through His Spirit at work in us.

You don't have to be a slave to your emotions. You too have a choice to make—likely each day, if you're anything like me. Will I surrender and open my heart to God's rule or let my emotions rule over me?

Choose today to walk by God's Spirit. Be honest with God about how you feel. And then let Him rule you rather than your emotions.

> Lord, search me and show me the areas of my heart that I am allowing too much control over my life. I confess those to You. I surrender to You. Come fill me with Your Spirit. Give me Your power to walk in the newness of life that is mine in Christ. In Jesus' name, amen.

ɞ In what way have you noticed your emotions ruling over you?

ɞ How can you begin to surrender to God's rule and not to your emotions?

....

....

....

....

73

Hot, Cold, or Lukewarm?

Karen

> *"I know your deeds, that you are neither cold nor hot. I wish you
> were either one or the other! So, because you are lukewarm—
> neither hot nor cold—I am about to spit you out of my mouth."*
>
> —Revelation 3:15–16

*L*awn chair? Check! Extra blanket? Check! Piping-hot drink to ward off any chill? Check!

It was opening day for my son's travel baseball team. I'd gathered all the components for a picture-perfect time and headed up to our town's ball fields. Now all I had to do was sit back and watch my boy throw strikes and hit balls while I hollered and cheered from the sidelines. (Yes, I am *that* woman!)

Just a few minutes into the game, I remembered I'd left my drink in the car. I trekked back to the parking lot to get it. When I got back to the field, I settled in my chair and took a sip of my custom-made latte from our local coffeehouse. How I'd looked forward to sipping on that hot drink on this chilly day! Only now it wasn't hot. It was lukewarm. And it wasn't very appetizing.

When it was hot, it was delicious. Why, even if it were cold, served over ice during a sunny, scorching July baseball game, it would be wonderfully refreshing. But now, in its middling temperature, it was bland and boring.

Today's verse tells us that God had the very same problem with the church in Laodicea. Because their faith was neither hot nor cold, but had turned a disappointing temperature of lukewarm, He was ready to be rid of them. While there are differing views of the interpretation of the temperatures hot and cold, Jesus' words are simple and clear: "I wish you were either one or the other!" (Revelation 3:15).

May we see today's verse as a challenge. Knowing that God has no need for lukewarm, may we seek to be those who offer refreshment and healing to a dying world. May our thoughts and actions not earn us the label of indifferent or ho-hum. After all, the God of the universe is on the sidelines watching us in the great game of life. May we please Him with our heart's desires and our actions done not to draw attention to ourselves, but only to point others to Him!

> Dear Lord, teach me to be intentional in my spiritual life and not complacent. May my words, thoughts, deeds, and actions please You and not be considered lukewarm. In Jesus' name, amen.

❧ Do you know someone who could use some words of refreshment from you today? Or how about words that bring healing to your relationship with them?

....

....

....

....

74

You Have a Calling

We have different gifts, according to the grace given to each of us.

—ROMANS 12:6

Many of us struggle to find our calling. It can seem elusive and hard to figure out, and many of us become discouraged as we seek to find it.

Thank goodness the Bible has a lot to say about callings! A calling from God is an invitation to return to Him. By faith, to respond to His grace and love in Christ. The most important calling is to be saved from our sins, forgiven, and declared acceptable and unconditionally loved by the God who made us. This is God's universal call—an invitation to everyone to come as they are, but not to stay as they are.

The Bible also talks about a more unique kind of calling, one that is specific to each of us based on the gifts God has given us. This includes our passions, experiences, education, skills, and God-given heart for a broken world. God has wired and given each of us a calling to help us steward our lives well for His glory and for the good of those around us.

You have something to offer the world. That's not only because you are great but because God is gracious. He is the One who has called you, will empower you by His Spirit, and will guide you into opportunities to love and serve others in Jesus' name. Yours might be a calling to lead and manage others. Perhaps it is the gift of serving behind the scenes. God calls us to show mercy and compassion to those who are hurting. We are called to teach. To give generously. To encourage and build up those who are discouraged.

Out of His goodness, God has chosen to accomplish His perfect purposes through imperfect people. He calls us to be with Him so we might represent Him to a watching world. Our lives matter. They are full of meaning and purpose because we have a God who loves us and has called us uniquely to be used by Him!

> Father, thank You for calling me into a relationship with You by faith in Jesus. I know You don't need me to accomplish Your purposes in the world, but You want me. You have wired me with gifts and abilities to be used for You and for the sake of others. Continue to show me the way You have uniquely made me and gifted me. In Jesus' name, amen.

- What are you most passionate about, and what gifts or skills have others in your church family affirmed in you?
- Do you have a gift that God is calling you to step out in faith and use for His glory?

....

....

....

....

....

75

Blank Screen Blessings

*My heart says of you, "Seek his face!" Your face, L*ORD*, I will seek.*

—PSALM 27:8

I pulled into the parking lot of our local fitness center with my usual grumpy attitude. You see, I hate to exercise. Oh, I love the way I feel when I'm done! But I still dread it every time.

Thankfully, the gym where I work out has flat-screens with cable television hooked to the various treadmills, bikes, and ellipticals. Members can view them to help pass the time. That is, if they remember to bring their own earbuds. This particular day, I did not.

Sighing audibly, I stepped onto the treadmill. How was I ever going to exercise for forty-five minutes or more staring at a blank screen rather than a news channel, like I usually did? That would be sheer torture. I'd get bored. I'd see the other people smiling and enjoying their programs while I got to look at a blank, flat piece of nothingness.

Then God brought to mind an area He had been nudging me in: prayer. By prayer I don't mean whipping out my list of jotted prayer requests and covering them all quickly before my head hits the pillow at night. I don't mean going mentally through my family members by name with the usual "bless 'em real good, Lord" request. I mean spending honest, focused, unhurried time just conversing with God about whatever is on my mind or on His. Perhaps my oversight in bringing my earbuds was the beginning of something good.

For the better part of an hour I imagined that Jesus was on the blank screen in front of me. He had my full attention. I tried to focus my mind on Him, what He was teaching me, and what things I still needed so desperately from Him.

In my mind I conversed with Him as with a dear friend. I poured out my thoughts. I shared my concerns. I asked Him to reveal to me my wrong attitudes and actions. All the while I pictured Him patiently there, listening and caring. I knew that time spent with Him would benefit me more than an hour of catching up on what was going on in the world.

Today's verse tells us to seek the Lord's face. That is exactly what I felt I was doing that day.

Could you spend some time seeking the face of the Father today— even if only for ten minutes or so—by tuning out all distractions and fixing your gaze only upon Him? It will be time well spent that will help you grow closer to Jesus and deepen your walk with Him.

Dear Lord, help me seize opportunities in my day that
normally would be idly spent to focus instead on You. I know
You are always waiting. In Jesus' name, amen.

  ❧ How often do you spend time in prayer without any particular written list or agenda, just pouring out your thoughts and concerns to the Lord like you would a close friend? Why does this sometimes seem foreign to us?

76

A House Full of Treasures

Ruth

By wisdom a house is built, and through understanding it is established;
through knowledge its rooms are filled with rare and beautiful treasures.

—Proverbs 24:3–4

*I*t's a vicious cycle. With four kids (including two teenagers), a large dog, and two hamsters, it seems like the minute we have the house clean, everything starts to come undone again! It's taken me years to be okay with not having the picture-perfect home.

There is nothing wrong with having a nice home. We should work hard to maintain the order and beauty of the space God has given us. But our goal should never be to have the *perfect* home.

I want my home to be a sanctuary, a place of refuge and rest for our family. I don't want to give in to the mess. But more important than having a house that is always clean and tidy is a home where God's presence dwells. After all, a home is to be lived in and not just looked at.

I love the reminder in the Old Testament book of Proverbs that says, "By wisdom a house is built" (24:3). We are to create and cultivate a home environment that honors God more than it impresses others. Instead of always filling each room with what looks good or is in style, we are to fill our house with "rare and beautiful treasures" (v. 4).

These "rare and beautiful treasures" are not material possessions, but spiritual blessings for our family. When we cultivate a home to be lived in for God's purposes, we are laying a foundation of faith. It's a home where Jesus is the center. It's a home where loving God and loving one another is the most important thing.

In a culture that values appearances, don't give in to trying to impress others. Seek to honor God with your home. Create an environment where God's presence is felt and His purposes are pursued. The influence that will matter most in your home is not how your house looks, but the One you are living for.

> Holy Spirit, come and fill my home. Make it a place of rest and refuge for family and friends. More than how it looks, remind me of the One I am living for. Teach me to build my home wisely, filling each room with the truth and promises of Your Word. In Jesus' name, amen.

❧ In what ways do you focus too much on how your house looks?

❧ What are some ways you can begin to fill your house with "rare and beautiful treasures" or blessings?

....

....

....

....

....

....

77

Tool, Toy, or Tangent?

Karen

My times are in your hands; deliver me from the hands
of my enemies, from those who pursue me.

—PSALM 31:15

J have a love-hate relationship with social media. I love that it keeps me connected to family and friends. It allows me to spy on ... er ... *keep up with* my kids, and I can post a prayer request when accidents or sicknesses occur. And I love reconnecting with some friends from my past. But I hate the way, if left unchecked and without boundaries in place, social media can become a massive black hole, eating up time and energy while diverting my attention from what's most important.

As a guideline I have learned to ask myself, *Is this a tool, a toy, or a tangent?*

The internet in general is a fabulous tool. It can be used for God and for good, such as organizing meals for a hurting family or participating in an online Bible study. But it can also be used for bad, including cyberbullying, extramarital affairs, and publicly and caustically airing our frustrations about other people.

It can also be a toy. Nothing is wrong with toys. We all need a little fun and relaxation. And if we enjoy playing games online, that's great.

What crosses the line is when any online activity becomes a tangent:

a sudden diversion that takes us off track from our priorities and responsibilities.

Tangents torch our time, sap our strength, and cause us to ignore loved ones. Tangents give us a false sense of being productive, doing *something*, when in reality, we aren't accomplishing anything. Then we feel frustrated, defeated, and even guilty when we realize how much time we've wasted.

In Psalm 31:15, the psalmist placed his time in God's hands and asked for deliverance from his enemies. Although he was speaking of physical enemies who could do him harm, we need to realize our tools, toys, and tangents can harm us too.

I've had my own tangents that have led me off track and caused me to neglect my family and household responsibilities. And these situations made me feel like a failure.

Maybe you have done and felt the same. Today let's prayerfully and carefully (with *all* honesty) ask ourselves while spending time online, *Is this a tool, a toy, or a tangent?*

By doing this and setting healthy boundaries, we can overcome the enemy of defeat and eliminate unnecessary frustration. We can free up time for the important relationships and tasks God has for us and live our lives in a meaningful, not frivolous, way.

> Dear Lord, teach me to use my time wisely, in a way that honors You and isn't derailed by tangents. I want to be efficient and effective for Your kingdom's work. In Jesus' name, amen.

∞ Reality check: How often do you let your time on social media become a tangent that is not helping you in life, but is actually

hurting you because it is causing you to waste many minutes—
or even hours—per day? It might be time to take some serious
action. Enlist the help of a friend who will keep you accountable
to refrain from the excessive use of social media. Or download
an app that will keep track of your time spent on these various
accounts and give you a wakeup call. (*Moments* is one such app.)
Write down your plan of action here.

....

....

....

....

....

....

....

....

....

....

....

....

....

....

78

Is Envy Stealing Your Joy?

Ruth

Rid yourselves of all malice and all deceit, hypocrisy,
envy, and slander of every kind.

—1 PETER 2:1

I scrolled mindlessly through my social media feeds. I was just passing time, waiting for my daughter to be done at the dentist. I glanced at pictures of vacations, friends celebrating birthdays, date nights, and a whole lot more. It's easy to see how quickly envy can invade the heart and steal our joy!

Envy is that sneaky and pesky desire to have what someone else has. It is the desire to possess something that doesn't rightfully belong to us. Envy can look like sorrow over a door closed to us but open to a friend or coworker. It might be a promotion we didn't get. Or perhaps we feel disappointment because of what appears to be someone else's healthier marriage or better-behaved kids.

We can be sure we are wrestling with envy when we notice feelings of anger, resentment, or even competition with others. But God desires for us something so much more. He wants a settled soul—a soul anchored in the goodness and grace of what He has done for us in Christ.

As the writer of Proverbs said, "A heart at peace gives life to the body" (14:30). There is joy and thankfulness with a settled soul. But "envy rots the bones" (v. 30). So how do we have a "heart at peace"? Start by ridding yourself of envy. We're envious when we always look at what we don't have, so we can fight it by focusing on what we do have and don't deserve.

Our joy and contentment isn't found in our circumstances. It's not found in how many friends we have or the things we possess. A heart at peace is anchored much more deeply. It is anchored in what God has done for us that we don't deserve. A heart at peace treasures Christ more than anything else.

Don't let envy steal your joy. Let the goodness and grace of God settle your soul.

> Father, You have given me so much more than what I deserve.
> Thank You for Your unconditional love, faithfulness, forgiveness,
> and hope. Guard my heart against envy. Instead, settle my soul
> by reminding me of all I have in You. In Jesus' name, amen.

❧ Where does envy tempt you the most?

❧ How can you begin to be grateful for what you do have and don't deserve?

....

....

....

....

....

79

Driven to Distraction

Karen

I called to the LORD, who is worthy of praise, and
I have been saved from my enemies.

—PSALM 18:3

Mom, quick—look at that lady!" my fourteen-year-old son shouted as we were headed down the interstate on an errand-running Thursday afternoon. "She should *not* be doing that," he added for emphasis.

I glanced over at the car next to us, expecting to see someone without her hands at the ten and two o'clock positions like my by-the-rulebook boy does when training behind the wheel. Instead, I nearly ran off the road while gawking at what he had spotted.

Next to us was a woman cradling her cell phone on her right shoulder, holding an open fast-food salad container in her left hand, ripping open a salad dressing packet with her teeth and her right hand . . . all while steering her car with her knees!

What in the world!? I thought. Surely if she kept up this multitasking method of driving, she was going to cause a crash.

I would never *attempt to do all of that when I drive,* I smugly thought to myself. *Entirely too dangerous and probably against the law.*

It wasn't until later that night it hit me. Yes, I may not dangerously multitask when driving, thereby risking collision. But in my day-to-day life? In my schedule? In my "sure-I-can-take-on-one-more-responsibility-so-everyone-will-like-me" way? I sometimes dangerously multitask to the point that I am headed for a crash.

Taking on too many responsibilities, no matter how "good" they may be, can often render us ineffective for service to God.

On one of my so-busy-I-couldn't-breathe days, I read today's verse. While I'm sure the author, David, was talking about actual physical enemies—people who could chase, catch, and ultimately hurt you—I realized that day my enemy was overcommitment. Too many activities and responsibilities were about to do me in. They chased me, cornered me, and, worst of all, were about to go in for the kill.

Thankfully, God can rescue us. He invites us to hold our too-full plates up to Him, allowing Him to scrape off any activities that aren't in His will. This lets us say no to multitasking and begin to focus on the things God may have for us.

When this happens, we can create space in our calendar to retreat and find sweet respite when we connect with God. Times when we slow down and sit still to listen and learn from the Creator of time itself.

So, how about it, friend? Let's start focusing on what God has for us *before* we crash and burn!

Dear Lord, forgive me for allowing busyness to overtake my life, crowding out others and, worst of all, You. Help me as I purpose to place only those items on my plate that You long for me to have. In Jesus' name, amen.

๛ Take a few moments to jot down all the commitments and responsibilities you have said yes to that are optional—meaning not a part of your home life or your employment if you work. Next, prayerfully look over the list, asking God if there are any you should bow out of because you no longer feel called to them or you only took them on in the first place because you have a hard time saying no.

....

....

....

....

....

....

....

....

....

....

....

....

....

....

80

Be the Kind of Friend You Are Looking For

Ruth

A friend loves at all times, and a brother is born for a time of adversity.

—PROVERBS 17:17

Over coffee, a woman I had been meeting with shared her frustration over not having formed any close relationships yet. She was new to our community and still settling in. I listened patiently as she gave several examples of how she didn't feel connected.

My heart broke for her because I know the power of friendships. In God's eyes, friendship isn't a luxury; it is a necessity! As we talked, I challenged her with something God had convicted me about years before. "What if instead of looking for the right friend, we started *being* the right friend?"

Friendships don't always come easy. They take time. And as life gets more hectic, friendships require intentionality. We have to make time to cultivate deep and meaningful relationships. Rarely do they just come to us.

So how different would our relationships be if we stopped looking for the perfect friend? What if we stopped trying to find that person we just really clicked with? What if, instead, we led with being the right kind of friend?

We probably all have that checklist of qualities we'd love to have in a friend. It's so easy to look for the right friend without seeking to be the right kind of friend. But friendship should start with us.

Be a friend who makes the first call.

Be the kind of friend who invites someone else out.

Be the friend who sends an encouraging text first.

Be the friend who asks questions and listens intently.

Be a friend who doesn't expect perfection.

Be a friend at all times, constant and available.

Start by being the right kind of friend. And watch what God does. I am convinced that many people are looking for meaningful relationships, but few are willing to be that kind of friend first.

Don't wait for someone else to come to you. Step out in faith today. Be the friend you are looking for!

Father, give me grace to love like Jesus today. Fill me with Your Spirit as I seek to be the right kind of friend. Help me sacrificially serve those around me and guard my heart against demanding from others what only You can give me. In Jesus' name, amen.

❧ How have you waited for the right kind of friendship?

❧ What is one way you can begin being the right kind of friend today?

....

....

....

....

81

Opening Doors Together

Karen

*From him the whole body, joined and held together by every supporting
ligament, grows and builds itself up in love, as each part does its work.*

—Ephesians 4:16

When my three children were small, we often went to the grocery store together to gather our needed fruits, veggies, and other assorted staples for the week. They especially liked going to one small grocery store in our town where an elderly man from church worked in the bakery. They lovingly referred to him as the "cookie man." They could hardly wait to get into the store and make their way back to the bakery so they could have a peanut butter or chocolate chip cookie to enjoy on our outing.

One spring afternoon the kids walked a bit ahead of me and reached the store's automatic door opener before I could. First, my oldest daughter, who was about eight years old at the time and somewhat small for her age, tried to step on the mat that causes the door to open. However, nothing happened. She stepped off, and then her younger brother, who was about five years old, tried too, also to no avail. Just then my daughter had a brilliant idea. She grabbed both her baby brothers' hands, and they all jumped on the mat together at the same time. Voilà! It worked! They needed their combined weight to make the door slide right open.

We as believers in Jesus need one another. Just as today's verse states, "Each part does its work" (Ephesians 4:16). Christians are not meant to be lone rangers; we're not designed to be islands unto ourselves. We are meant for community. When members of the body are in need of something—whether physically, spiritually, financially, or emotionally—God most often sends help in the form of another human to lighten their load, relieve their pain, or encourage their heavy heart. Or when someone needs to figure out the next steps to take in life, God uses others to help think through decisions, weigh options, and make the best choice.

When we offer our help with all these life issues and join hands together as siblings in Christ, we can open doors we might not be able to open on our own.

Be willing today to take the hand of another person to help them get to where he or she feels God is guiding them to go. Will you play the part God has chosen for you in the body of Christ? When you do, the results are even sweeter than an afternoon treat from the cookie man himself!

> Father, please help me be attentive to those around me who might
> need me to take them by the hand to help them get somewhere.
> I want to play my part and represent You well. It is an honor to
> have a place in the body of Christ. In Jesus' name, amen.

༜ Can you think of a situation where you might join along with someone to help them get where they are headed? What could you do to come alongside them today?

82

Done Complaining

Ruth

The people complained about their hardships in the hearing of the Lord, and when he heard them his anger was aroused.

—NUMBERS 11:1

We complain about the weather. Bad traffic. Long days at the office. We grumble about our spouses or about being single. You name it, and we find a reason to talk about it and feel frustrated because of it. Complaining is so commonplace in our culture.

But it seems that God takes complaining far more seriously than we do. Why? Because the real source of our complaints is not our circumstances; the real source of our complaining is our attitude toward God. So while complaining doesn't always seem like a big deal to us, it is to Him.

The Bible's record of the Israelites being rescued out of Egypt and then wandering in the wilderness is a great example of how easy it is to lose sight of God and give into grumbling. On numerous occasions, shortly after seeing the goodness and power of God show up, His people quickly forgot. They started making assumptions about God and accusations toward Him.

They complained about not having enough food (Exodus 16). And then when water appeared to be in short supply, they grumbled about that too (Exodus 17:1–7). Nearly a year later, after setting out from Mount Sinai, the Israelites "complained about their hardships" (Numbers 11:1) such that the Lord could hear them. To be clear that God is not indifferent to our complaining, the writer explained that God heard them and "his anger was aroused."

So what's the big deal about complaining? While our circumstances may very well be hard, if not tragic, complaining often reflects a blindness to God's abundant grace and faithful promises. Complaints question God's love, presence, and purposes. And many times our complaining is really questioning whether God knows what He is doing. The problem with our complaining is not our hardships; it is with our heart.

Today, whatever circumstance you find yourself in, remember how good and faithful God is. Meditate on what you have been given! God is good. He is faithful. Your soul can be settled in Him.

> I praise You, Lord, for You have been good to me. You are faithful, and Your love endures forever. Forgive me for the times when I lose sight of who You are and all You have done for me. Guard my heart from grumbling against You. In Jesus' name, amen.

- In what ways does complaining show blindness to God's grace and faithfulness?
- How does gratitude guard your heart against grumbling?

....

....

....

83

Get Yourself Together

Karen

Seek the Lord, all you humble of the land, you who do what
he commands. Seek righteousness, seek humility; perhaps
you will be sheltered on the day of the Lord's anger.

—ZEPHANIAH 2:3

Recently while clicking around online looking for houses for sale, I happened upon a site for foreclosed homes. One such home was in a nearby town our family was considering moving to, so we hopped in the car to drive by and take a look.

We pulled into the neighborhood and found the home at the end of a cul-de-sac. Suddenly it hit me. I'd seen this house before! When it was built more than twenty years ago, it was featured in the local parade of homes. But the house that stood before me now was not at all one to be showcased. It was in a state of severe disrepair with overgrown, scraggly landscaping and a dilapidated, sagging roof. It looked almost uninhabitable. A neighbor who saw us looking at it warned us it was overrun with rodents.

But someone must have seen past the ramshackle state of this property because last month it went back on the market. It had been completely gutted and remodeled and now sported all the latest must-have renovation items such as shiplap, sliding barn doors, and a huge farmhouse kitchen sink.

Zephaniah chapter 2 tells of God's calling His people to get their act together because their nation was in a state of disrepair. This prophet urged them to repent while there was still time, allowing God to cover and conceal their sins.

Just as the Lord told wayward people in the Old Testament to gather together and repent, we must get ourselves together—through the power of the Holy Spirit—who can enable us to walk in obedience. The dilapidated home that was converted back into a showpiece again could not renovate itself. Neither can we. We can, however, allow God to do the transforming as we cooperate by humbling ourselves, seeking Him, desiring to walk in righteousness, and obeying His commands. We can make time for studying His Word and connecting with Him through prayer. We can purpose to care about our spiritual growth, making it a priority in our schedules.

When we do our part by getting ourselves together, God sees our willing hearts. Then He acts with His incredible power and allows us to be wonderfully renewed.

Father, may I not take sin lightly but instead examine it seriously in light of the awful grip it can have on me, causing devastation. Help me seek righteousness, pursue humility, and follow Your commands. In Jesus' name, amen.

❦ Is there an area of your life that needs an overhaul? If so, which of these actions from Zephaniah 2:3 do you most need to do: seek the Lord, obey His commands, pursue righteousness, or acquire humility?

....

....

....

84

Chasing Donkeys

Ruth

Kish said to his son Saul, "Take one of the servants
with you and go and look for the donkeys."

—1 SAMUEL 9:3

As soon as the Israelites asked the prophet Samuel for a king like all the other nations, we meet a young man named Saul. In the beginning of 1 Samuel 9, Saul was completely unaware that he was about to be anointed the first king of Israel. What he *was* made aware of was that his dad had lost some family donkeys and he needed Saul to help with the search.

These must have been some valuable donkeys because young Saul and a servant searched high and low. They searched the hill country of Ephraim and the area around Shalisha—but no donkeys. They searched in the district of Shaalim—yet no donkeys. Then they went to the territory of Benjamin; still they found no donkeys. Finally, they reached the district of Zuph, and—you guessed it—no donkeys. That's when Saul wanted to turn back. I can only imagine that he was tired of looking everywhere for a few donkeys.

But at the servant's suggestion, they continued to a nearby town to look for a man of God who would give them guidance on where to find these lost donkeys. Little did they know that this man of God was

Samuel. And little did they know that the Lord had spoken to Samuel the night before regarding Saul. Samuel assured them that not only had the donkeys been found, but God's man, the next king of Israel, Saul, had been found too (1 Samuel 9:20).

Saul had no idea he was headed right to the man God would use to appoint him king. He was just out looking for some donkeys. While there is a lot we could say about this passage of Scripture, we can at least conclude that sometimes when we are "chasing donkeys," the Lord has a lot more in store for us. We never know why we are being asked to be obedient in some area of life. And sometimes we never know where our obedience will take us or what God will do with it.

So whatever the Lord is asking you to do, no matter how big or small, whether it makes sense or not, regardless of whether anyone sees it, be faithful. Persevere. Don't be afraid to chase those lost donkeys!

> Lord, I want to trust and obey You. Help me be faithful in all things—
> big and small. I know You want to do far more with my life than I
> can even imagine. Give me grace to surrender to You for the sake
> of Your glory and purposes in my life. In Jesus' name, amen.

❧ How can you learn to be obedient even with the small things of your life?

....

....

....

....

85

When Others See You in the Storm

Karen

All the sailors were afraid and each cried out to his own god.

—JONAH 1:5

My friend, Cindy, and I sat stunned in our seats as our flight began its final descent to the airport. The pilot had just announced that there was a possible malfunction in the landing gear and it could be jammed, unable to open properly. He instructed us to tighten our seatbelts and assured us emergency vehicles would be on the runway ready to help if there were trouble.

My heart raced as I feared for us. But by God's grace, the landing gear became unstuck, and we landed safely.

A group of seafarers had a similarly scary trip on an ancient ship headed to Tarshish, which is likely modern-day Spain. On the vessel was a passenger named Jonah. Yes, that Jonah—the one who wound up inside the belly of a big fish after he ran away from God and failed to do what He'd asked him to. Once Jonah was aboard the ship, the Lord caused a mighty storm that lurched the ship brutally upon the crashing whitecaps. The valiant mariners, who were used to sailing in storms, became tremendously frightened, each crying out to his own god.

When the idols did not answer, the seamen took matters into their own hands, flinging cargo overboard to lighten the boat. But neither the squall nor their anxieties subsided. They then cast lots to see which passenger onboard had caused the storm. When it fell to Jonah, he fessed up about being a runaway, urging them to promptly toss him overboard.

The sailors didn't do it at first; instead, they rowed all the harder. Finally, they granted Jonah's request. When the storm instantaneously waned, they were overwhelmed by God's enormous power, offered a sacrifice to Him, and pledged to serve Him from then on.

The sailors started out fearing the storm. But finally, these rough-and-tumble guys stopped fearing the elements and began to fear God instead when they witnessed Jonah choosing to admit his fault and do what was right.

How might others in your life—who are in fear of their circumstances and futilely placing trust in false things—come to fear and revere God when they see you acting in obedience today, even in the midst of whatever storm you're currently caught in?

Father God, may I not run the other direction when You ask me to obey. Empower me to make godly choices and use my obedience to point others to You no matter the storm I am facing. In Jesus' name, amen.

❧ Are you are facing a storm in life right now? Use the space provided to write out a prayer to God asking Him to help you choose obedience in the midst of the turmoil and use your behavior to help others to revere and worship Him.

....

....

....

86

Putting on Patience

Ruth

*As God's chosen people, holy and dearly loved, clothe yourselves
with compassion, kindness, humility, gentleness and patience.*

—COLOSSIANS 3:12

I can still hear my grandmother's voice echoing in my ear, "Patience
is a virtue, Ruthie!" It didn't matter what we were doing: Cooking
in the kitchen. Assembling a puzzle. Driving to the swimming club. My
tendency toward impatience was always met with her gentle reminder
that patience is of great value.

In the New Testament, we are often encouraged to "be patient"
(Ephesians 4:2). In Colossians 3:12, the apostle Paul described the Christian
life like clothing with some character qualities, attitudes, and actions we
are to discard like an old garment. Instead, we are to "clothe" ourselves
with something better, more beautiful. "Clothe yourselves," he wrote,
with "patience" (v. 12).

Patience enables us to respond to all life throws at us in a God-honoring
way. Our circumstances often reveal our hearts' sinful tendencies and
desires. Sometimes our impatience can reveal our pride, need for control,
need to be right, or lack of faith that God is good and faithful.

We have patience, or respond in a God-honoring way, when we
are slow to anger. When we are willing to forgive, make room for one

another's faults, and wait in hope for God to come through (Psalm 33:20–21). When we are unsure of God's faithfulness and wise involvement in our lives, we will have no patience.

Where are you struggling to be patient? How is God using your circumstances to reveal what is really going on in your heart?

As God continues to grow us and change us from the inside out, He produces in us "love, joy, peace, forbearance, kindness, goodness, faithfulness, gentleness and self-control" (Galatians 5:22–23). Our goal is to reflect who God is. He is a God who is slow to anger and abounding in love. As we fix our eyes on Jesus, opening our hearts to His love and truth, He clothes us with something far more attractive—He gives us patience.

> Father, thank You for being patient with me. You love me unconditionally. You are gracious with me. Help me respond to others the same way You respond to me. In Your name I pray, amen.

❧ What does impatience reveal about your heart?
❧ What is one way you can pursue patience in your relationships?

....

....

....

....

....

....

87

Standing Outside the Door

Karen

Peter stood outside at the door.

—JOHN 18:16 ESV

*H*ave you ever been somewhat reluctant to identify yourself as a Christian? Perhaps it was because you were afraid someone might ask you a question about the Bible that you didn't know the correct answer to. Or maybe you've witnessed some very judgmental and unloving behavior from others who say they are people of faith and you were afraid to be lumped in with them.

On the final night of Jesus' life, we see another believer who was afraid of what others might think of him if he identified himself with Jesus: the apostle Peter.

Earlier in John's gospel, we see Peter confidently declaring that Jesus possessed the words of eternal life (John 6:68). He even brazenly stated that he was willing to follow Jesus so closely that he would lay down his life if necessary (John 13:37). But Peter's words and his sword wielding soon stop short when, just a few pages later, we read of his shrinking back and lurking in the shadows instead.

Peter denied that he knew Jesus three different times (John 18:17, 25, 27). This fulfilled Jesus' prediction in John 13:37–38 (ESV) where He told

Peter, "Truly, truly, I say to you, the rooster will not crow till you have denied me three times."

What happened to make this once-bold disciple begin to separate himself from the Lord he claimed to love so loyally and stand outside the door in John 18:16 rather than right by Christ's side? Other gospel reports depict Peter's backing away that night by declaring that he followed Jesus from a distance (Matthew 26:58 and Luke 22:54).

Why did Peter's fearlessness fizzle? Perhaps for the same reason ours does sometimes today. We fail to see in the natural unfolding of earthly events what God is doing in the spiritual realm. If we truly understood, we'd cease fighting, stick closely by His side, and trust Him instead.

To listen—and respond—to the truth of Christ, we must be close enough to hear Him speak through His Word. This hearing of His Word doesn't happen when we stand outside the door, following from a distance, afraid to be identified with Him. It happens when we throw wide open the doors of our hearts, let His words settle deeply into our souls, and courageously trust Him with the future. The best way to do this is to spend time reading, studying, and even memorizing scripture in an attempt to align our attitudes and actions with the Word of God.

Father, help me stop standing outside the door, afraid to identify myself with You. I don't want to lag behind, watching from a distance. I want to follow so closely that I can hear You speak to me through Your Word. In Jesus' name, amen.

✿ Do you feel as if you are in some ways standing outside the door in your relationship with Christ? What is one practical step you can take today to help draw you closer to Him?

88

Dealing with Disappointment

Ruth

You can make many plans, but the LORD's purpose will prevail.

—PROVERBS 19:21 NLT

J had a plan. I knew exactly how many children I wanted. I had grown up dreaming of having a very large family with at least six kids. I had it all figured out. The problem was that my plan was different from God's. After several miscarriages, I found great joy in the miracle of the four children God had given me. But I would be lying if I didn't admit I felt grief and disappointment that I couldn't have more.

We dream. Make plans. Sometimes we wait and hope. But often our dreams do not come to fruition. The vision we had for our future shatters, or at the very least, is different from what we were planning.

It might be a job. The size of our family. Health. Moving to a different city. A dating relationship or spouse. No matter the plans we make and the dreams we dream, inevitably we will experience disappointment. Why? Because not all of our dreams are God's desires. As the Bible reminds us, He has a purpose for our lives that is far greater than our plans.

And so we learn to surrender. We hold loosely the things we desire and dream about. We remember that our lives are ultimately for God's glory. Not all our ways are His ways. He knows better. He understands more. He is writing a story in which we are not always privy to how all the parts work together.

But even more than that, we need to remember that God is the greatest treasure. He is the greatest reward. He alone is the fullest satisfaction of our souls. As the apostle Paul said, "I consider everything a loss because of the surpassing worth of knowing Christ Jesus my Lord, for whose sake I have lost all things. I consider them garbage, that I may gain Christ" (Philippians 3:8).

Any satisfaction we could get from our plans and dreams will never come close to knowing God and being known by Him. He is of supreme worth. Disappointment can be a gift because it drives us closer to God.

Open your heart, asking the Lord to fill you with the joy and satisfaction that only He can give you.

> Lord, teach me to delight in You. I surrender all my plans and dreams
> to Your will. I want You more than anything. Come and change all
> of me, aligning my heart to Yours. In Your name I pray, amen.

- ❧ In what circumstances have you experienced disappointment?
- ❧ How can disappointment reveal the things you treasure more than God?

....

....

....

....

....

89

What Is Your Plumb Line?

Karen

*This is what he showed me: The Lord was standing by a wall that
had been built true to plumb, with a plumb line in his hand.*

—AMOS 7:7

When our children were growing up, they knew my husband
and I had certain expectations for them when it came to
their behavior. We required them to address adults as *ma'am* or *sir*. We
expected them to be on time for meetings and events. If we ever got a
little pushback from one of our kids, questioning why they needed to
behave a certain way, we always gave them the same answer: "Because
you are an Ehman."

God has expectations for us as His children as well, and He desires
that we behave in keeping with what is outlined in His Word. The Old
Testament prophet Amos wrote about these expectations, both those
that God had for individuals and those He had for society at large.

In today's verse, the prophet saw a vision of a plumb line. At the time,
a plumb line was a thick cord weighted at one end with a lump of lead.
It was held up to the top of a structure with the weighted end near the
ground. As gravity pulled it downward, it made the cord straight. Then
builders were able to check whether vertical structures were perfectly
straight.

The image of a plumb line is used symbolically here to refer to the godly standard against which the Lord would measure the behavior of His people. He had found Israel and its leadership to be chronically crooked, so the nation would be judged harshly.

We can glean a few concepts for our lives—and our behavior—from the vivid account of this vision.

God has standards. Yet He hasn't left us to fend for ourselves, trying to figure out how to live our lives here on earth. His Word is our plumb line, and in it we find instructions for living as well as cautions for what might happen when we disregard His directives.

Each of us has a response to His standards. We have a choice in life. We can decide to follow God and obey His commands, or we can scrap His standards and make up our own guidelines. Each choice has its own consequences.

Even when we choose wrongly, the Lord's mercy triumphs over His judgment. God is prepared to grant mercy when we humbly ask for it. And His ultimate act of mercy was in sending Jesus, His only Son and the one true prophet, to offer us forgiveness and save us from eternity spent apart from Him.

Praise God for both His plumb line and His mercy when our behavior fails to measure up.

Father, may my only plumb line in life be Your holy Word. Help me study it, understand it, and be quick to obey its commands. In Jesus' name, amen.

❧ While God's Word should be our ultimate plumb line, for many in our culture, this is not the case. What are some other things

you're tempted to measure yourself against to determine if you
are successful in life?

....

....

....

....

....

....

....

....

....

....

....

....

....

....

....

....

90

Seeing It Through

Ruth

*I have fought the good fight, I have finished
the race, I have kept the faith.*

—2 TIMOTHY 4:7

Assembly projects don't go so well in my house. We start with great enthusiasm and just about call it quits thirty minutes later when we realize how difficult the TV cabinet or desk is to put together. We always manage to finish, but it's not easy!

A story in the Old Testament book of Numbers reminds me that between starting and finishing, it's in the "middle" when we often find it most difficult to endure and remain faithful. The writer described the stages of Israel's journey out of their slavery in Egypt. Step-by-step we're told how they started, progressed, and finished. I love the picture we find in Numbers 33:3. We're told that "the Israelites set out from Rameses on the fifteenth day of the first month, the day after the Passover. They marched out defiantly in full view of all the Egyptians."

At the beginning of their journey, they "marched out defiantly." They were ready to go. Energized for the trek. Confident of the Lord's deliverance and direction. At the beginning, they were most enthusiastic about walking with God. And yet we know their confidence and defiance didn't last long.

They would grow discouraged. Confused by what God was doing, they would question their decision to step out in faith. They would grumble, complain, and eventually wish they could turn back toward where they came from. They were great at the start, but not so good at the middle or end, wandering way longer than they had to. A strong commitment to endurance would have served them well.

Endurance is a theme we see throughout the Bible. Toward the end of his life, the apostle Paul reflected on his journey of faith and proclaimed, "I have fought the good fight, I have finished the race, I have kept the faith" (2 Timothy 4:7). While far from perfect, he had endured, remained faithful, and experienced the goodness of staying the course.

Where is God calling you to stick it out? Have you started something with great enthusiasm but are now struggling to endure? Don't give up, my friend! Don't miss what God has for you by quitting too soon.

Father, make firm my steps. Keep me from growing weary in what You have called me to. Give me Your grace not only to start well, but to remain faithful. Teach me to humbly walk in faithfulness so I might finish the task You have called me to. In Jesus' name, amen.

- What are you most tempted to quit right now because it's hard?
- Where do you believe God is calling you to stay the course?

....

....

....

....

91

Sprinkled In but Set Apart

Karen

*"My prayer is not that you take them out of the world but that you
protect them from the evil one. They are not of the world, even as
I am not of it. Sanctify them by the truth; your word is truth."*

—JOHN 17:15–17

Have you ever heard the old saying that asserts, "Christians are to be *in* the world but not *of* the world" and wondered what exactly is meant by that concept? To fully understand it, we need a little English grammar refresher course.

Two different prepositions are used in this saying—*in* and *of*. If you are *in* something, it refers to your setting—where you're physically placed. If you are *of* something, it means not just near in proximity, but that your very being finds its identity in it.

This ancient adage has its origins in our passage for today as Jesus Himself addressed this concept in His prayer for His disciples—both the ones in the New Testament as well as all who would come to follow Him.

In His prayer the Lord addressed the tension that exists in dwelling physically here on earth while also refraining from adopting the mind-set and habits of the world. He didn't ask God to take His disciples out of the world, but rather to sanctify them in truth while they continued to dwell here on earth.

The original Greek word *sanctify* used here means to set apart, be different, and be consecrated. It also indicates being pure, in stark contrast to things that are profane.

Jesus didn't pray for God to isolate His followers, forming their own exclusive Christian club. He asked Him to make them stand out in contrast to the world because of their behavior. Just as the brightly colored sprinkles on the top of a birthday cupcake stand out *from*—but are not melted *into*—the buttercream frosting they top, so believers are sprinkled into the world but are to remain separate from it in behavior.

God, through the Holy Spirit, can empower us to live in this world, rubbing shoulders with those who do not know Him while still being visibly different from them in our moral behavior. He will enable us to live in a way that displays the truth of the gospel to those who are watching us. May they observe our set-apart and sanctified ways and desire to know more about the one true God we serve.

Father, please help me exhibit behavior that is set apart and different from that of the world with behavior that represents You well. In Jesus' name, amen.

෪ Have you ever struggled—either now or in the past—with navigating the tension of being *in* the world but not *of* it? Describe the situation, and write a short prayer asking God to help you be set apart in both your beliefs and your behavior.

....

....

....

92

What Anger Reveals

Get rid of all bitterness, rage and anger, brawling
and slander, along with every form of malice.
—EPHESIANS 4:31

Not all anger is wrong. But in most cases, whether in the workplace, relationships, or marriage and family, our anger can lean in the direction of unrighteous anger—the sinful and self-seeking kind. This is what the apostle Paul was warning against in Ephesians 4:26 when he wrote, "In your anger do not sin." The anger God has instructed us to "get rid of"; not some, but "all bitterness, rage, and anger" (v. 31).

The truth is, our anger says a lot more about what is going on inside of us than what is being done to us. Unrighteous anger exposes our selfish and sinful desires. And God wants us to get rid of unrighteous anger because it is destructive to our own souls and has the power to damage the relationships we hold dear.

So how do we allow the Holy Spirit to reveal what change is needed in our hearts? One way is by asking God to show us the selfish and sinful desires that are really driving our actions. The stuff we want more than loving God and loving others. We get angry when we don't get a promotion at work. We grow resentful toward a friend who doesn't see things our way. Traffic is moving slowly. Our kids aren't being quiet enough.

We get another interruption when we are trying to focus on something important. Each of these can disrupt what our hearts really want—control, comfort, the need to be right, and so on. The problem with most of our desires is that they are focused on us.

What is the real cause of your anger? Let God search you and expose those desires of your heart that are bent inward. God wants to replace unrighteous anger with something better—He wants to produce in you love, joy, peace, patience, kindness, goodness, faithfulness, gentleness, and self-control (Galatians 5:22–23 NLT). Will you let Him?

> Father, search me and reveal to me the areas I am struggling with right now. Give me understanding into what is really causing my anger. I repent of my selfish desires. Create in me a heart that desires to honor You and love others more than myself. In Jesus' name, amen.

- What sinful desires are most often at the root of your anger?
- What is one way you can "get rid of anger" today?

....

....

....

....

....

....

....

93

The Color of Love

Karen

If you really keep the royal law found in Scripture, "Love your neighbor as yourself," you are doing right. But if you show favoritism, you sin and are convicted by the law as lawbreakers.

—JAMES 2:8–9

I sat in the quaint Southern café that afternoon, spreading honey on my piping-hot biscuits. My adult daughter and I had taken her three-year-old goddaughter, Naomi, who is Ethiopian, to meet a friend and her seven-year-old daughter, who is also Ethiopian by birth. The girls colored with crayons on placemats while the three of us adults visited.

At one point during the meal, my friend's daughter reached her arm over by mine to grab a napkin. I noticed we both had on shirts that were the exact same shade of teal green. "Look, Aster! We match!" I observed, stretching my arm out toward hers so she could see our identically colored shirts. A puzzled look came over her face. It was then that I knew what was happening.

Slowly, she pulled up her sleeve, revealing her beautiful ebony skin. She then touched my pale arm, shook her head, and said, "No, we don't." My heart sank. I meant that our shirts matched. She thought I was talking about our skin.

I have become increasingly aware of how often I fail to see life and situations from the eyes of those who do not share my race. Or those who are marginalized, left out, or weary from how society treats them. While my, "Look! We match!" assertion was an innocent oversight, the little girl's reaction has adhered to my heart as a reminder not to always see the world from my own point of view, whether racially, economically, ethnically, or otherwise.

Today's Scripture passage from James sums up the royal law: love your neighbor as yourself, and don't show favoritism (2:8–9). These are always the right things to do. Oh, we may argue that we *do* love and *don't* play favorites, but often the partiality is subtle—such as in thinking that our ethnicity, race, or life situation is the default without giving thought to the other person's perspective and experience.

Let's begin today to be ever mindful of even the slight ways we might make others feel insulted when we aren't sensitive to the particulars of their life's journey in our culture today.

> Father, You do not show favoritism but offer salvation to all regardless of race, gender, ethnicity, social status, wealth, or ability. May I be sensitive to both the plights and the feelings of others and treat them with the love and respect that is in keeping with the royal law. In Jesus' name, amen.

ॐ What can you do this week to reach out and show love and acceptance to someone who is different from you in life experience, race, religion, or ethnicity? Spend a few moments praying for love and understanding in our culture that will fight against favoritism.

94

Standing in Awe

Ruth

Let all the earth fear the LORD; let all the people of the world revere him.

—PSALM 33:8

ave you ever watched someone do what seems impossible and found yourself in awe? Our family loves the Olympics. During the last Winter Olympics, we watched several sports we don't typically watch, including the luge. Some have described this sport as sledding down an icy mountain at ninety miles per hour. Not exactly my idea of fun, but we were amazed at how people had learned this sport. We marveled at their ability to remain positioned on their sled while winding down an icy track at extremely high speeds. You could say we were in awe.

What is awe? Awe is when we are overcome with a sense of wonder, reverent fear, and appreciation. I often question, with our busy and active lives, if we have lost our sense of awe. In particular, awe of God. We are easily entertained, but are we easily enthralled by God?

When I read the Bible, I am reminded that when people truly encountered the power and presence of God, they couldn't help but be moved. They were filled with wonder. Awestruck. Worship was the only rightful response.

If we are in Christ, to fear God, as mentioned in Psalm 33:8, means to esteem Him. It is to hold Him up and see Him for who He really is. To fear God is to treasure Him. To stand in awe of Him.

With all that life throws at us, we can quickly become consumed, indifferent to the presence and power of God around us. It is so easy to get distracted. Overwhelmed with busyness, work, family, and kids' activities. One of the greatest risks to us in crazy and chaotic seasons is to have an underwhelmed soul.

Have you lost your sense of awe? Are you feeling underwhelmed? Slow down today. Be still. Get away to a quiet place. Don't just read God's Word; meditate on the truth and promises of God. Think deeply about all Jesus has done, is doing, and will do someday. Don't let your soul be underwhelmed. Stay in worship until God meets you, bringing awe that overwhelms and settles your soul.

> I worship You, Lord. You alone are worthy of praise. Quiet my soul today. Fix my eyes on You. Show me the wonders of Your love. Satisfy and strengthen my soul today with Your power and presence. In Jesus' name, amen.

∞ Describe a time when you were in awe of God.
∞ What is one way you can begin slowing down to pay attention to who God is?

....

....

....

....

95

IRL Over URL

Karen

*Perfume and incense bring joy to the heart, and the pleasantness
of a friend springs from their heartfelt advice.*

—Proverbs 27:9

I recognized the familiar buzzing sound as my cell phone did a vibrating dance across my kitchen island, signifying another notification coming through on social media.

I stopped what I was doing—folding laundry while also trying to catch up on the latest news from my neighbor—to check my phone to see what the latest pings and dings were all about. A new follower on Twitter. A private message on Facebook from someone. A few likes on an Instagram image I'd put up just minutes prior.

When I'd finished clicking and tapping my way around all the latest notifications, I looked up. My neighbor was headed out my front door and back to her house across the street. I'd allowed the pull of my phone to eclipse the flesh-and-blood person standing right in front of me!

The abbreviation IRL stands for "in real life" and is used to denote a person you know in the real world, not just the world of the internet. The acronym URL means Uniform Resource Locator and is used to specify addresses on the internet. What often happens in our phone-driven culture today is that we let the places a URL may take us—to a blog, social media site, or comment thread—supersede the time spent with people we know in real life—family members, neighbors, friends, or coworkers. As a result, our IRL relationships stagnate, suffer, or even stop developing altogether.

Today's verse speaks of the pleasantness of heartfelt advice from a true friend. Oh sure, we can cultivate online friendships that are helpful and even deep, but there is just something so spiritually satisfying about a friend who knows you up close and personal—one who can help you in times of uncertainty, confusion, or sadness. Face-to-face connections with people with whom we share life in close proximity can grow, deepen, and encourage us in ways that exhibit what the Bible refers to as fellowship—a heart-to-heart bond with other believers that comes from the shared common love of the gospel of Christ.

So put down your phone. Find a real-life relationship you've been neglecting and reconnect. Together you can share life, offering support, advice, and maybe even a neighborly cup of coffee sometimes.

Father, forgive me for the times when I let the pull of technology trump the call to connect with the people You have placed in my actual life. I want to do better. Help me put IRL people over the buzzing and beeping of my phone. In Jesus' name, amen.

∞ Evaluation time! On a scale of one to ten, with one being never and ten being always, how often during the day do you succumb to the tug of technology? What self-imposed guidelines can you follow to stop letting apps and sites take time away from the people in your life with whom you should be connecting instead?

96

Envy's Enemy

Ruth

From that time on Saul kept a close eye on David.

—1 SAMUEL 18:9

Not long after young David killed the Philistine giant, Goliath, King Saul took him into his home. The Israelites' fear and dread of their enemy had disappeared in an instant when David, then a young shepherd, picked up a few smooth stones and silenced Goliath for good.

Things were going well for David. He was young, handsome, victorious in battle, and now residing with the king and his family. Things were going *too* well. For it wouldn't take long for King Saul to begin growing suspicious, insecure, and envious of David's successes in battle.

On one occasion, as David was returning from another win on the battlefield, he was met with a chorus of praise: "Saul has slain his thousands, and David his tens of thousands" (1 Samuel 18:7). King Saul took note not only of David's win but his own successes compared to David's. In verse 9, we read that "from that time on Saul kept a close eye on David." In other words, Saul became envious of David.

King Saul was unable to celebrate David's success. He wanted the praise that rightfully belonged to David, and as a result, he became envious. He kept a "close eye" on him.

This is how envy works. It is always comparing, competing, desiring, and watching. Envy wants what belongs to someone else. Envy is often blind to what God has given us that we don't deserve. Envy steals our joy. Distorts our perspective. Snuffs out our gratitude. And it can even make us an enemy of those around us. This is exactly what happened to Saul, as the writer told us in verse 29, "Saul became still more afraid of him, and he remained his enemy the rest of his days."

Who are you keeping a "close eye" on in your life? Is there someone you are secretly envious of? Have you made someone your enemy? Take your eyes off that person, and fix your eyes on Jesus. Remember all you have in Him. Delight in all He has done for you that you don't deserve. Let gratitude fill your heart so you can love others instead of competing with them!

Jesus, You are my greatest treasure. You have done far more for me than I deserve. Guard my heart against envy. Help me keep my eyes on You. Fill me with joy and gratitude. Forgive me for wanting what doesn't belong to me. Give me grace to humbly love You and love others. In Jesus' name, amen.

ↄ Where have you noticed envy in your life?
ↄ How has envy caused you to secretly compare and compete with someone?

....

....

....

....

....

97

Fret Not Yourself

Karen

> *Be still before the LORD and wait patiently for him; do not fret when*
> *people succeed in their ways, when they carry out their wicked schemes.*

—PSALM 37:7

I tried distracting myself by flipping through an old magazine in the orthodontist's waiting room. However, no barbecue meatloaf recipe, insightful article on how to organize my closet, or column on the Hollywood gossip scene could keep my mind from worrying. An acquaintance was spreading lies about one of my family members as if they were factual. I was both angry and anxious and grew more fearful by the moment that some people—who might not know my relative well—would believe the lies.

My mind began to concoct all sorts of short speeches and clever comebacks I might give if I spoke with anyone who had been the recipient of the untruths. However, into my mind popped a piece of advice my spiritual mentor, who had introduced me to the gospel in high school, had repeated to me numerous times: *Remember, the truth always wins out, and it is God's job to protect your reputation. It is your job to stop worrying and trust Him with the outcome.*

Oh, how this is easier said than done! I wanted to correct the errors, straighten out the untruths, protect the name of my loved one, and stop the person who was lying! However, today's verse suggests just what my mentor told me: "Do not fret when people succeed in their ways, when they carry out their wicked schemes" (Psalm 37:7). And what are we to do instead? The first part of the verse: "Be still before the Lord and wait patiently for him."

Do. Not. Fret. Or, as the King James Version of the Bible puts it, "Fret not thyself." I just love the picture that rendering paints! It shows that *we* are the ones causing ourselves to fret, and so *we* are the ones who can stop "fretting ourselves," for crying out loud! We just need to be still. To wait. To display patience, the quiet trust that God is in control.

My mentor was right. The truth did win out. My family member's name was cleared, and the person spewing the lies instead was the one who ended up looking foolish and bad.

If you are fretting, take the advice of Psalm 37:7 today and fret not yourself. You'll be glad that you did.

> Lord, whenever I begin to feel anxiety rising up in me over the harmful words or actions of another, help me to stop. To pray. To trust in Your plan and leave the fretting behind. In Jesus' name, amen.

∞ Think back on a time when it felt like someone was succeeding in his or her wicked ways. How could Psalm 37:7 have helped you handle that situation differently? How can it equip you for any future fretting that might come your way?

....

....

....

98

You Don't Have to Be Rich to Be Generous

She opens her arms to the poor and extends her hands to the needy.

—PROVERBS 31:20

*I*f I had a dollar for every time I warned my children to "watch out!" I'd be a rich woman. "Watch out for traffic," I tell them when crossing the street to get our mail. "Watch out for your little sister!" when the boys are wrestling. "Watch out, turn the channel, this is a bad commercial!" when we are watching TV. And the list goes on. What mom, out of love and concern, doesn't feel like she is constantly telling her children to be careful?

Jesus was no stranger to telling His disciples to "watch out!" either. On one particular occasion, He said, "Watch out! Be on your guard against all kinds of greed; life does not consist in an abundance of possessions" (Luke 12:15). Many sins are easy to see in our hearts or lives. But Jesus said greed is much harder to identify. That's why we are told to "watch out" for "all kinds of greed." We don't always notice its presence or power, but greed can plague anyone. So to fight it, we need to develop generosity.

When Jesus told the story about the poor widow in Luke 21, He praised her, even though she gave little in comparison to the rich. She gave out of her poverty (vv. 1–4). Like the widow, we can be generous, even with very little. How? Because it's how we give and not just what we give.

What God desires is a generous heart that delights in giving freely and often. After all, this is how God has loved us in Christ. Spiritually we are poor, yet in Christ, we are now rich. God has blessed us in every way. The good news of what God has done for us motivates us to live more generously with others.

Where are you struggling to be generous? Whether it is with your money, your time, or the gifts God has given you, "watch out" that you don't just use them for yourself!

Jesus, You have been so generous with me. You have not been stingy with Your love. Give me grace to love and serve others in the same way. Guard my heart from being greedy with my time, talent, and treasure. I want to live with an open heart and open hands, blessing those I come in contact with. In Your name I pray, amen.

- Where do you struggle most with generosity? Is it with your time, treasure, or talent?
- What is one way you can be generous today?

....

....

....

....

....

....

99

Heavenly Minded *and* Earthly Good

Karen

*Just one thing: As citizens of heaven, live your
life worthy of the gospel of Christ.*

—Philippians 1:27 csb

Once when I was a teenager playing softball on our church's team, I overheard a conversation describing another church member. Our left-fielder had declared, "Oh, she is almost so heavenly minded that she's no earthly good!" It made me wonder, is this old saying in fact true?

It reminds me of my friend, Thida. She's a natural-born citizen of Cambodia who relocated to the United States when she married Keith, an American. I had the pleasure of not only attending their wedding reception, held here in the States, but later writing a recommendation letter for her when she applied for US citizenship.

To officially become a citizen, Thida had to study diligently to become well versed in American history and the laws of the country. Once she'd passed the exam and the committee had reviewed her recommendation letters, she was ready to make it official. Thida's smile stretched wider than the Golden Gate Bridge when she became a full-fledged citizen of the US. However, even though legally she's now American, she remains a natural-born citizen of Cambodia too.

We Christians are also dual citizens. Though we dwell here on earth, we should be ever cognizant of the fact that most importantly we are citizens of heaven. What we think and how we act should reflect this direction: "As citizens of heaven, live your life worthy of the gospel of Christ" (Philippians 1:27).

We are celestial citizens inhabiting earth. As dual citizens, our practice should be to study God's Word to make sure we take our heavenly citizenship seriously. Will others be able to vouch for us, confident that we are believers who represent the kingdom well?

As we share Jesus' love and carry out the commands of Scripture, it makes us more compassionate, helpful, encouraging—more concerned about justice and caring for the poor, marginalized, and ostracized.

Let's remember today that our aim is to live lives worthy of the gospel of Christ—ones that draw others to Him when they see our loving behavior.

May we be both heavenly minded *and* do earthly good.

Dear God, I am living here on earth as a foreigner. Help me not become too wrapped up in the ways the world does things. Help me continually place my treasure and hope in heaven as I reflect the gospel to a watching world. In Jesus' name, amen.

❧ In what ways are the world's ways of thinking and doing things foreign to you? How have you gotten too comfortable here? How can you fix your eyes back on heaven, your one true home?

....

....

....

100

Pursue Joy

Ruth

Restore to me the joy of your salvation.

—PSALM 51:12

For many people, living each day with joy is a struggle. We often wait or hope joy will come to us, but the Bible tells us to be joyful and be glad in God. But joy is something we pursue, not something that pursues us.

So how can we pursue joy? We will never truly experience real and lasting joy apart from pursuing our Father, who loves us and delights in us. And we pursue Him by eliminating that which comes between us. Biblical joy is the fruit of walking with God. It is a byproduct of an intimate and growing relationship with the Father, through Jesus, by the power of His Spirit. We can't have one without the other. When we pursue and enjoy God for who He is, the Holy Spirit produces joy in us.

But it is a joy that must be protected and cultivated. Lots of things in life can steal our joy. Psalm 51 is a great reminder of an often overlooked thief of joy: sin. Raw and honest, in Psalm 51, King David confessed his sin. His guilt had grabbed his joy because his sin had come between him and his God.

David cried out, "Restore to me the joy of your salvation" (Psalm 51:12). Sin disrupts the joy we experience when walking humbly and faithfully with God. Willful and unconfessed sin in our lives, whether it be our attitudes or actions, interferes with the intimate relationship we are intended to have with God.

Psalm 16:11 says, "You make known to me the path of life; you will fill me with joy in your presence." God wants to give us life and fill us with His joy. While our sin doesn't sever our relationship, it does disrupt our intimacy and the experience of God's abundant joy.

Is it possible that your struggle for joy is really a struggle of the heart? What if God wants to begin cultivating more joy in your life, not by changing your circumstances, but through confession?

Today ask God to search your heart, revealing any sinful desires that might be stealing your joy. Pursue God. Seek His presence. And watch how He produces joy in you!

> Father, restore unto me the joy of Your salvation. Search and know me. Reveal any sin that might be stealing my joy. Fill me with Your presence that I might increasingly experience the abundant life You offer me in Jesus. In Your name I pray, amen.

- ❧ Where do you struggle the most with joy?
- ❧ What sin do you need to confess that might be stealing your joy?

....

....

....

....

About Karen Ehman

*K*aren Ehman is a Proverbs 31 Ministries speaker, a *New York Times* bestselling author, and a writer for First 5, a Bible study app that reaches more than 2 million people daily. She has authored fourteen books, including *Keep It Shut: What to Say, How to Say It and When to Say Nothing at All*, *Let. It. Go.: How to Stop Running the Show and Start Walking in Faith*, *Keep Showing Up: How to Stay Crazy in Love When Your Love Drives You Crazy* and *Pressing Pause*, coauthored with Ruth Schwenk. Karen has been featured on numerous media outlets, including FoxNews.com, Focus on the Family, Redbook.com, Crosswalk.com, and *HomeLife* magazine.

Karen has been married for over a quarter-century to her college sweetheart, Todd, and together they raise their three sometimes quarrelsome but mostly charming children in the boondocks of central Michigan. There she enjoys antique hunting, farmers market strolling, and processing life with family, friends, and the many teens and young adults who gather around her kitchen island for a taste of Mama Karen's cooking.

Connect with her at KarenEhman.com, where she helps women to live their priorities and love their lives.

About Proverbs 31 Ministries

If you were inspired by *Settle My Soul* and desire to deepen your own personal relationship with Jesus Christ, I encourage you to connect with Proverbs 31 Ministries.

Proverbs 31 Ministries exists to be a trusted friend who will take you by the hand and walk by your side, leading you one step closer to the heart of God through:

Free online daily devotions
First 5 Bible study app
Online Bible studies
Podcast
Daily radio program
Books and resources

For more information about Proverbs 31 Ministries,
visit www.Proverbs31.org.

About Ruth Schwenk

*R*uth Schwenk is the founder of the popular blog The Better Mom and, along with her pastor-author husband, TheBetterLifeMinistry. org, which is home to TheBetterMom.com, ForTheFamily.org, and RootlikeFaith.com. She is the trusted author of several books, including *The Better Mom* and *The Better Mom Devotional*, as well as *For Better or For Kids: A Vow to Love Your Spouse with Kids in the House*, coauthored with her husband. She also, together with Karen Ehman, coauthored *Hoodwinked: Ten Myths Moms Believe and Why We All Need to Knock It Off* and *Pressing Pause.*

Ruth is a Michigan football superfan, a self-proclaimed "foodie," and a lover of all things HGTV. But her greatest joy is her family. She lives with her husband, four children, two pesky hamsters, and their loyal Labrador retriever in the beautiful college town of Ann Arbor, Michigan.

HEY, MOM. YES, YOU!
COULD YOU USE SOME CALM IN THE CHAOS?

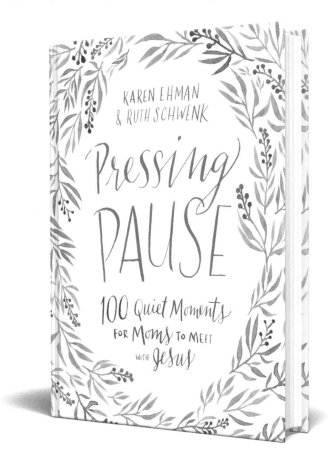

KAREN EHMAN
& RUTH SCHWENK

Pressing
PAUSE

100 Quiet Moments
FOR Moms TO MEET
WITH Jesus

Whether you're juggling a career, kids' schedules, and church commitments or you're covered in spit-up and anxious about what the next 18 years might hold, perhaps it's time to press pause.

AVAILABLE WHEREVER BOOKS ARE SOLD.

 ZONDERVAN®